"A friendly and thorough guide t[...] every woman living a cram-jamm[...] *The Everywoman's Guide to Persona[...]* space of our own. In a world with lots of noise and little quiet, the personal retreat becomes a countercultural—and life-giving—choice. Let Letitia Suk walk you through your doubts, fears, questions, and reticence. Don't wait. Get the book and get away with God. Your soul—and all the people in your life—will thank you."

> **Jane Rubietta**, international speaker, author of 19 books, including *Resting Place: A Personal Guide to Spiritual Retreats* and *Worry Less So You Can Live More*

"Have you ever thought, *I need to get away and take a retreat with Jesus?* Then all those counter thoughts hit you: *How will I spend the time? Where will I go? How can I fit anything else in? How can we afford it?* Letitia Suk, out of the rich meditative practices of her life, has provided the answers to all your concerns in this wondrously meticulous guide. The book is part gentle wisdom shared by an experienced and gifted life mentor and part remarkable memoir drawn out of the author's own life, and it addresses any and every question that could be raised by those of us who think, *Should do but how to?* I have been stuck for two days due to weather systems trying to get home from Dallas to Chicago, but thanks to Letitia, I am making this a spiritual retreat and am now sitting in the sun with almost no one near me but Jesus. Thank you, Letitia. *Getaway with God* is a gem!"

> **Karen Burton Mains**, director of Hungry Souls

"As women, we can get so caught up in taking care of others and in our to-do lists that we lose track of nurturing the most important relationship of all—the one with God. This book is a gentle, beautiful invitation to say yes to the Lord's invitation to come with him to a quiet place. Letitia provides step-by-step instructions to those who desire them, but also encourages women to find their own retreat path. She shares her own journey with humility and grace. It's a book any woman at any stage of life or spirituality will learn from and savor."

> **Melanie Rigney**, author of *Blessed Are You: Finding Inspiration from Our Sisters in Faith*

Getaway with God

The EVERYWOMAN'S GUIDE *to* PERSONAL RETREAT

....

Letitia Suk

Getaway with God: The Everywoman's Guide to Personal Retreat
© 2016 by Letitia Suk

Published by Kregel Publications, a division of Kregel, Inc., 2450 Oak Industrial
Dr. NE, Grand Rapids, MI 49505.

All rights reserved. No part of this book may be reproduced, stored in a retrieval
system, or transmitted in any form or by any means—electronic, mechanical,
photocopy, recording, or otherwise—without written permission of the publisher, except for brief quotations in reviews.

Distribution of digital editions of this book in any format via the Internet
or any other means without the publisher's written permission or by license
agreement is a violation of copyright law and is subject to substantial fines and
penalties. Thank you for supporting the author's rights by purchasing only
authorized editions.

All Scripture quotations, unless otherwise indicated, are from the Holy Bible,
New International Version®, NIV®. Copyright © 1973, 1978, 1984, 2011 by
Biblica, Inc.™ Used by permission of Zondervan. All rights reserved worldwide.
www.zondervan.com

Scripture quotations marked MSG are from *The Message*. Copyright © by Eugene
H. Peterson 1993, 1994, 1995, 1996, 2000, 2001, 2002. Used by permission of
NavPress Publishing Group.

ISBN 978-0-8254-4415-9

Printed in the United States of America
16 17 18 19 20 21 22 23 24 25 / 5 4 3 2 1

To Thomas,
for always believing.

And my granddaughters,
Aaliyah, Lydia, and Camila,
to start you on your way.

Come with me by yourselves to a quiet place
and get some rest.

JESUS (MARK 6:31)

CONTENTS

ACKNOWLEDGMENTS

My heart is full of gratitude for so many who have been cheerleaders for me along the parade route for this book, including . . .

The Write-to-Publish Conference staff, Lin Johnson and my dear friend Jane Rubietta.

My editor at Kregel, Steve Barclift.

My writing coaches, Robin Stanley and Ginger Kolbaba.

My mom, Betty Wiewel, who taught me how to pray and first took me to the ocean.

My women's group, who prayed through every draft and sigh: Theresa Decker, Pat Dinges, Alison Doo, Cathy Ellison, Eloise McDowell, and Cindy Nicholson.

The small groups of women who have come along on my group-guided personal retreats to try on the concepts.

My four beloved children and their families: Jeshua and Jessica, Gabriel and Kimberly, Selah and Ignacio, and Christa Joy.

Tom, always Tom, whose love and support daily sustain me.

To Jesus: thanks for the invitation. Glad I RSVP'd yes.

DEAR FRIEND

What if you could plug your soul in for a long recharge like you do your phone every night? If you're like me, the "juice" on my phone can slide into the red zone without me even noticing. An emergency-like response sets in as I desperately grab the charger to plug back into the power. Staying connected to the source feels critical. And that's just for a phone.

Our souls work like that too—draining constantly throughout the day, even more during times of crisis. As with the phone, we may not be aware of the energy loss until we are nearly empty.

How do you know when you are skirting into the red zone? See if you can answer yes to any of these questions:

> Are you weary of the rush to the next day?
> Do you feel stretched edge to edge?
> Are you overbooked and overwhelmed?
> Do you rarely leave room for margin in which to refuel?
> Do you long for time to just *be* with God?

I'm raising my hand and so are countless other women, whether busy moms or active executives, new believers or lifetime church members. "I need time with Jesus" echoes in small groups, on social networking sites, in coffee shops, and in blog posts. We're all hungry for a soul recharge: extended time alone with God.

In spite of the expressed need, life totally gets in the way, and the timeless remedy of just getting up a little earlier to fit it all in is no longer effective. In fact, most of us try and try to squeeze in time for Jesus and finally quit, feeling like failures. We long for more, but we're out of ideas about how to attain it. Sound familiar?

Getting away with God on a personal retreat works like that overnight charge. We plug into the source of all life and let him fill us to the brim. One full charge can last a long time as we resume the race set before us. Hope returns, peace floods in, and the mental fog lifts. Something about hanging out with the creator of the universe brings things into perspective.

Enticed but skeptical, right? Don't worry, I'll address your concerns; I've had them all myself. *Getaway with God: The Everywoman's Guide to Personal Retreat* tells my story and invites you to begin to write your own. Come along with me. I will show you the way to the renewal and spiritual intimacy you long for. You'll be ready for an encounter with God that can fill you with more joy and blessing than you've imagined could be yours.

Ready? Pull up a chair.

Warm regards,

Tish

PS: In the early stages of writing this book, I stopped by a party my neighbor threw for her girlfriends. I didn't know anyone else there, but the host and I engaged in conversation with a woman I met. Instead of the usual chitchat, she began telling me how she occasionally attends church and is figuring out her own faith. She felt a strong need to "get away" on a retreat type of experience to sort it all out. She brought it up, not me.

I laughed inside at God's timing and then filled her in on my passion for inviting women to do just that: get away and sort it all out. My new friend told me to hurry up and write the book. It truly seemed like a divine encounter to both of us.

This book is for her and you and all the women who long to get away with God and need a girlfriend to show them the way.

PART 1

You Can Do This!

Chapter 1

HOW IT BEGAN

An Introduction

Like many of us, I already spend a few weekends a year retreating: family retreats, all-church retreats, small group retreats, women's retreats, and marriage retreats. By definition, a retreat offers time to come away from the day-to-day demands and focus on our relationship with God.

Common themes usually include singing, plentiful (and sometimes good) food, inspiring messages, and *lots* of people. Retreats provide great opportunities for strengthening relationships, renewing vision, and letting someone else cook for a change. Usually we return home feeling encouraged, energized, and probably in need of some sleep.

Now, I love the girlfriend time at the retreats, the laughing, the skits and snacks, and the teachings. Some women freely admit to really not caring who is teaching; they just like leaving home. But while most of my weekend experiences enriched my relationships with my family and friends, time *alone* with God at these events often seemed minimal and tacked on at the beginning or end of a long day.

In spite of all the fun and great camaraderie, I often still felt in need of a retreat.

In the early years of our young church, I attended one of these large group retreats at a local convent. While browsing the book area, I picked up a brochure for the facility and noticed "Private retreats available" listed among the amenities. Right away I was intrigued, but I was unsure what a "private" retreat would be. The idea suggested an unhurried time to pray, read, and just enjoy being with God at my own pace.

I was ready to sign up, but I felt clueless about how to spend twenty-four hours without a retreat schedule in hand. So I stuck the brochure in my bag and took it home.

A few months later, while seeking God about the direction of my life and not hearing much back, I pulled out the brochure. Immediately, myriad questions flooded my mind:

If I do this, will I just pray the whole time?
Should I fast?
What does it mean to "wait on God"?
What if I get bored?
How spiritual do I have to be to try this?

Then the possibilities began to emerge—time *alone*, time to really seek God, a chance to finish that Bible study I started at the beginning of the year, an opportunity to sort out the next season of my life. Way too much agenda for one retreat. I called the facility and made a reservation.

For the next nearly thirty-five years I went back once or twice a year. First to that convent until it was torn down for a housing development. Then other places. Some years I went to a bed-and-breakfast; other times, to a friend's empty-during-the-day apartment. The "where" wasn't as important as just showing up to hang out with Jesus.

Time after time, year after year, I came away filled with a renewed sense of purpose, clarity of vision, trust in God's ability to untie all the knots of my life, and an overwhelming sense of being loved. Can you see why I kept making the reservation? Part 1 of this book tells you step-by-step how to design and experience your own short retreat so you can enjoy similar benefits.

Fast-forward to six months into my sixtieth year. I wondered how God viewed my life so far. I still anticipated the full actualization of all his plans for me, but life was moving fast, and I yearned for an opportunity to take a long look at where I had been and where I was headed.

My journals of the previous few years reflected common transitions in this season of life: the launching of children, family weddings, the death of a parent, some dreams realized and others laid to rest. The journals contained my angst about stuck points in my life and my wonderings about what was next.

I longed for a chance to identify themes in my life's journey as well as plan for what I hope will be several more decades of service to God's kingdom and deep enjoyment of life. But that process never seemed to fit into a Sunday afternoon. Turns out I didn't have to cram it into a few hours as God invited me to spend five luscious days away with him for some of the most transformative moments of my life. But now I'm getting ahead of myself . . .

Chapter 2

THE BASICS

Answering Your Questions

Clutching my overstuffed suitcase in one hand while balancing my purse and additional "just in case I have time" bag in the other, I managed to wrest a hand free to ring the bell of a large retreat facility near my home. The year was 1977, and I was on the doorstep of my first personal retreat, carrying plenty of excitement, a bit of anxiety, and way too much stuff.

In the early evening, I had driven about thirty minutes to the same convent where my church had its retreat. This time, though, instead of heading to the group area, the nuns directed me to their newly renovated wing set aside specifically for personal retreats. This section contained nine small rooms, each furnished with a bed covered with a colorful spread, a small desk and chair, another comfy chair for sitting, plenty of light, and a sink. Decorative touches and new carpeting added to the inviting atmosphere. Down the hall was a lounge area set up like a large living room, and a common bathroom.

I have always enjoyed having some lovely personal space, and this fit the bill perfectly. The sister who led me to my room invited me to walk the grounds, visit the chapel, and help myself to tea and cookies in the basement snack room anytime. I did all the above.

I arrived after dinner (no fasting) but planned on eating breakfast and lunch the next day with any other retreatants in the private dining room. Turns out I was the only one there. When I showed up for breakfast, a plate of hot, delicious food awaited me along with a pot of hot water for my tea. I saw no one come or go, so it was like the angels had dropped off the provisions.

I spent the rest of the morning praying, reading, journaling, and walking through the beautiful grounds in the back among apple trees and grapevines. I was surprised but delighted to see that the same angels had dropped off my lunch, as once again I saw no one else around. After lunch I took a nap and then another walk. I spent the last hour of my first retreat reflecting on my time there and the new perspective on my life I had gained from it. The twenty-two hours away felt like two weeks, and I couldn't wait to come back.

Thirty-five-plus years of personal retreats later, I want to invite you to come along. I hope you can envision us having a cup of tea together while I share with you more of my story and fill you in on how delightful a getaway with God can be.

What Is a Personal Retreat?

You probably have a few questions, so let's start with those.

I like the definition Ben Campbell Johnson and Paul Lang offer in their book, *Time Away: A Guide for Personal Retreat*: "Retreat is a temporary withdrawal to be renewed, to regroup, and to find the strength you need to go forward."[1] The *personal* part means you go by yourself. This is more than an afternoon free time at your church's annual women's retreat.

Getaways with God are not just for the "super-spiritual" girls. In fact, if you want to go on a retreat just to get some time alone, that's okay. Don't confuse a retreat with a vacation, though. A retreat beckons you to snuggle up with God and let him love on you. Save the shopping and movie watching for another time.

This is not a "nun for a day" program; it is an intimate time hanging out with the One who knows you better than anyone else and loves you like crazy. Try thinking of your personal retreat like a spiritual spa. Doesn't that sound inviting? For a day or two, you check yourself into a place to rest, pray, listen to God, feel his love, take a walk, and enjoy a nap or two.

While most women I know would drool at the opportunity to have even an afternoon off from their responsibilities, somehow the notion of actually making it happen can be somewhat intimidating. Beloved women of God who would not hesitate to take a day of shopping if someone offered often have a hard time taking that very same time to go on a retreat. Perhaps it's because the concept seems so mysterious. But the rewards of a retreat last much longer than the new items purchased at the mall.

Why Do I Need One?

Most women need an urgent care facility for their weary souls. Busyness, fatigue, family issues, and work crises stack on top of each other like a pile of the old-fashioned pick-up sticks. We can get good at detangling the demands from time to time, but not for long. One set of emergencies flows into the next, and even the quiet days can be fraught with anxious thoughts.

A lot of women are sure some break in the schedule is just a week or two away. As soon as the kids are either out of school or back in, or the project at work is finished, or we take our vacation, or we get home from our vacation, or the renovations are done, or the paper gets turned in, or the campaign is over . . . *then* we can take a break. We all know how that usually works out. A whole new set of circumstances is waiting in line—and the break gets put off once again.

Caffeine breaks, chocolate, and trips to the mall are like taking an aspirin for a migraine. Taking a personal retreat, on the other hand, is like hooking up to an IV of grace and rest. Nothing is more restorative than spending a day with Jesus and feeling his love.

Sure, a lot of women can get by without a personal retreat. But are you a "get by" girl or a "go after" girl? Ladies, we are responsible for our own spiritual practices. Our pastor, husband, mom, or friend can't make our renewal happen. Just as it's up to us to read our Bible, only we can orchestrate a day or two away with Jesus.

what other women have to say

"I love going on personal retreats, because it is extended time with just me and God with no distractions. It's a chance to rest in God's presence, read his Word, pray, and journal for extended uninterrupted periods of time. It's also a chance to hear from him without the distractions of life."—Janice

"I am involved in intense, demanding ministry with traumatized, homeless, and exploited women in an impoverished inner-city neighborhood. I need retreat time on a regular basis to rest and hear from God."—Julia

"We often separate body and spirit during the day, and personal retreats are wonderful, necessary ways to unite those two again so we can live as whole, connected people."—Cheryl

Where Do I Go?

Many venues can work for a getaway with God. The essential component is space to be alone without interruptions. My first few years of taking retreats led me back to the previously mentioned Catholic convent. Sadly, the convent eventually came down so new homes could be built. My friends and I still grieve the loss. Fortunately, other area convents and monasteries still exist, and I visit most of them.

If you are on a tight budget, a convent or retreat facility usually fits the bill for anonymity and few distractions. Check the website or call ahead to see if they serve meals and if special requests can be accommodated. Do they have a fridge available for you to bring your own meals? Is there a place to walk? Is silence the norm? Appendix E provides a list of links for retreat centers.

Sometimes you might prefer a hotel-like environment. A dear friend of mine waits for the winter hotel specials in Chicago and plans her retreat for that time. I discovered a charming bed-and-breakfast about an hour's train ride from my home that became my retreat venue for a few years. Silence was not to be had, but there was a lot of quiet.

For a no-cost retreat, consider asking a friend who is gone during the day if you can use her place, or trade homes with a friend for a weekend. When my children were starting morning programs in school, I asked a neighbor from church if I could use her apartment for a morning retreat while she was downtown at work. I didn't have the luxury of an overnight or even a full day, but the change of venue and close proximity created just the place I needed.

An outside retreat at a public garden, large park, or on the beach can work in the right kind of weather for a shorter retreat. Bring along something comfortable to sit on and create your own sacred space.

One word of caution: Staying home to retreat may seem like an ideal solution. But if possible, get out of your house. Too many distractions of undone chores, ringing phones, and chicken to thaw out for dinner can derail the best of plans.

what other women have to say

"I have found it easiest to connect with the Lord and quiet myself if I am somewhere other than my home. There is a spirituality center out in the country, about seventy miles from my house. I went there for part of Thanksgiving last year. That to me was perfection. So quiet you could hear crickets, so dark you could see the stars at night, so alone, other than with the Lord."—Melanie

"I decided to take my retreat at a hotel in Michigan. I wanted to be by the lake, wanted to go to a place I knew, and wanted to travel less rather than more."—Jean

How Do I Get Ready for a Retreat?

Preparing for a retreat is just like getting ready for any other trip. Some women never end up going because it seems like too much trouble, but it doesn't have to be. Careful planning, as with any other event or project, can simplify the process of leaving.

I have found these steps helpful to prepare for my retreats:

1. Start a conversation with those who would be most affected by your absence: your husband, children, roommates, and employer. Of course, if you are taking a one-day retreat, there will likely not be much change in the day-to-day.

2. Unless you feel a compelling reason to go NOW, choose a time that fits relatively well with the rest of your life. There will be no perfect time to go, so don't wait more than a week from your decision to book a place. Often it works well to plan the retreat a month or so out, when your schedule looks more open, and then book other events around it.

3. Make arrangements for your absence. Just as with any trip, provide for the needs of your family, pets, and colleagues. Provide an emergency number, but clarify that it is for a true emergency, not a chat. I know—that's a hard one for those of us who are so used to being available 24/7.

4. Choose your transportation. Are you driving? Taking public transportation? Getting a ride with a friend? Walking or biking? Decide how you want to get there, and have a backup plan in mind in case of car repairs or weather changes.

5. Enter into spiritual preparation. I didn't realize how important this step was when I first started taking retreats; I never miss it now. As soon as you schedule it, commit your retreat

to God, and ask him to begin preparing you for what he has planned. It is a good idea to ask a few others to also be praying for your retreat, as getting away with Jesus invites spiritual opposition. Extra prayer support before, during, and after your retreat can be essential to your experience.

Now that some of your questions have been answered, let's talk about what kind of retreat might best fit your needs.

packing for a personal retreat

In addition to your usual packing list, these are some other items you may want to take on a personal retreat:

❖ Bible
❖ Bible study materials
❖ Notebook
❖ Pen (or assorted colored pens)
❖ Journal
❖ Inspirational book
❖ Music, headphones
❖ Walking shoes/attire
❖ Water bottle
❖ Meals/snacks
❖ Additional reading material for breaks/bedtime
❖ Small items to personalize room such as photos

Chapter 3

ONE STYLE FITS ALL

Not!

A re you on Facebook, girlfriend? I jumped on a few years ago, and oh my, can I get lost scrolling and scrolling through page after page of photos. These aren't just my photos; they're all the photos of all my "friends" as well, and sometimes even their friends. You get caught up too?

Have you noticed the variety of vacation photos among favorite posts? Families with young children flock to beaches. Traveling to renowned cities seems popular for couples in early seasons of marriage. Adventure shots of camping, hiking, and other strenuous activities pop up on my more intrepid friends' posts. Isn't it fun to travel vicariously to so many different vacation spots in a single afternoon?

Just as vacations come in many different styles, retreats do too, depending on our personality or season of life. What fits one season might not be as life-giving in another. What suits one friend's personality might not fit yours.

In this chapter, I'll offer you a "menu" to help you choose the best retreat option for wherever you are right now. Just like at a restaurant, take a sip of water, settle in, and read all the possibilities before making your choice. Ready?

A Restorative Retreat:
What If You Just Want to Take a Nap?

When my dear friend Gail was in the early years of raising children, she never seemed to get a mommy break. Her toddlers didn't nap, her parents both had health issues, and her husband worked long hours. After hearing repeated stories of my personal retreats, she asked wistfully if she could come along next time. (More on this in the next chapter.) I knew we would both stick to our own agendas, so I said, "Sure."

The day I picked her up, she strolled from the house with a very small bag slung over her shoulder. Surely, I thought, she'll need to go back in for another bag. But she glanced at my overstuffed suitcase on the back seat and climbed into the car, all ready to go. (Okay, so I have a hard time downsizing when it comes to packing.)

"Where is all your stuff?" I asked. "Your books, pencils, and notebooks?"

"Oh, I'm planning to take a bubble bath, a long nap, and maybe a walk," she answered, patting her little bag. "I have everything I need in here."

I must admit to feeling a little shocked as well as somewhat judgmental. Didn't she remember the stories of insights I got at my retreats from reading and writing? How could she call this a retreat if she was just going to rest?

My friend took her naps and her bubble baths, and I read and wrote. Funny, but we both came away feeling very satisfied with our time away. Different strokes for different folks.

Many years later, I finally understand the simplicity with which my friend approached our side-by-side retreat. *Rest* can be a primary retreat agenda. And rest looks different for different people. I learned that from living with my husband, who finds raking leaves restful.

A retreat that offers time away to be with God as well as a time for deep rest is called a *restorative retreat*. This type of retreat focuses on nutrition, sleeping often, drinking lots of water, and simply experiencing the presence of the Lord without doing much else. But before you sign on the dotted line for this one, let me unfold it a bit more.

This restorative retreat is often chosen by moms in the season of rearing young children. I often called this season of my life the "blur years." I remember little about it except that the intensity of parenting excluded almost every other aspect of life. (Oh, and I sure remember the week the kids all got chicken pox.) My verse of the day for *every* day pulled me through: "He gently leads those that have young" (Isa. 40:11).

It is hard to get away from young children for any length of time, because there is always one more thing to do. And besides, you're too tired to even think about planning dinner much less a retreat.

Exhaustion, the major side effect of this season, often distorts our perception of ourselves as well as of God. Catching up on sleep at home isn't likely to happen for a long time. Someone once told me you don't get your energy back until your youngest child is four. For a mom of multiple children, a long wait might ensue. My youngest child turned four and the next one was born ten days later. Back to "go" to start the count all over again.

Okay, so maybe you're not a young mom or a mom at all. Still exhausted? I thought so. Did you ever think the green pastures and quiet waters God uses to restore our souls (see Ps. 23:2-3) might look like your private room at a personal retreat? Or dining on a nutritious meal or two that you don't have to plan, prepare, and clean up? Don't you feel the restoration seeping in just thinking about it?

In case you are still wondering whether resting counts as a real retreat, look at the story of Elijah in 1 Kings 19:5-8. After one of the most triumphant, as well as trying, points in his ministry, Elijah is full of self-doubt and doomsday thinking: *I have had enough, Lord.* He then collapses into a long nap until he is awakened by an angel, who offers him food and drink.

Elijah eats the catered bread, drinks the water, and falls back to sleep. Once again the angel wakes him with more food and water. Then "strengthened by that food," he travels a long distance to do the next thing on God's agenda.

Doesn't it seem possible that God might want to offer you something similar for your weariness? The correct answer is yes. Perhaps you're willing to admit the need for deeper rest, but maybe you're struggling, as I did, with the bubble bath idea. Good thing Queen Esther didn't question bubble baths or she might never have gotten around to becoming queen.

"Before a young woman's turn [to audition for queen] . . . she had to complete twelve months of beauty treatments prescribed for the women, six months with oil of myrrh and six with perfumes and cosmetics" (Esther 2:12). God is so surprising sometimes.

Are you sufficiently enticed? If you're hitting the wall—if you're looking for the toothpicks to keep your eyes open—start with a restorative retreat. You'll thank me later.

what other women have to say

"One long weekend I spent most of my time in the prayer chapel listening to worship music and letting it wash over me. It was a very good time. Sometimes I sleep a *lot* and then don't have enough time to spend just soaking in God's presence. Sometimes I try to learn or read or "take in," and realize I don't have the energy for that. I need to somehow balance my need for rest with my need for spiritual restoration and refilling."—Julia

"I did get time to rest on my retreat—go to bed early, be still, just be. I was excited to feel like God was inviting me to be there, that he felt tenderness toward me, that he loved me and had good things for me."—Darilyn

"On my first retreat I realized that I was ready for bed at 8:00 PM Having the freedom to do that, guilt-free, was amazing."—Julie

A Listening Retreat:
Will God Speak?

Most of us would love to sit down with Jesus for an intimate conversation and get all our questions answered. Especially if we're assured we aren't in any kind of trouble, right?

Scripture is full of stories of God speaking to his people in such a way that they clearly knew it was his voice. Sometimes, as with the words of the prophets to Israel, the message was for a large group of people. At other times it was more intimate; think of the personal words God brought to Hagar, Samson's parents, Zechariah, Mary, and others. Words of endearment, instruction, comfort, or direction all flowed to God's loved ones as needed.

Most of us don't need convincing that God speaks to people. We just aren't sure he will speak to *us*. Guess what? He wants to speak to you, and he has a lot to say when you take time to listen. Getting away with God on a personal retreat can provide the time, place, and space to sit with Jesus and listen deeply. Don't expect a booming "Thus sayeth the Lord"; listen instead for a still, small voice whispering in your ear. Not that God couldn't speak out loud, but most of the time he speaks through the words of the Bible.

That might make you flinch a bit because there are parts of the Bible you haven't read or don't understand. True confession: I don't understand it all either. But there won't be any pop quizzes on the retreat. You can even just page through a portion of the Bible and see what shows up. God can be very creative in getting our attention.

Is there a book or chapter of the Bible you have been longing to dig into? A theme that keeps coming up for you, such as "don't be afraid" or "the peace of Christ"? Maybe you would like to know more about ess, hospitality, or the fruit of the Spirit? Sometimes I run into a concept I would love to research, and I make a note of it for my next retreat.

How about a character study on one of the Bible celebs such as Ruth, Daniel, or Mary? What notable trait keeps you remembering a particular individual? Courage? Faithfulness? Obedience? You may not have time this week to study such a person, but you would on a retreat.

If you would like to use some existing resources, an abundance of Bible studies are available on any of the above topics and many more. Stroll through your local Christian bookstore, or search Internet sources such as BibleGateway.com. And prepare to be overwhelmed by all the choices—I always am. Take your time, pay attention to key words or themes, and you will be able to narrow down your search and pick just the right tool for your season.

You can also transport yourself back to the day when none of these resources were available, only your Bible and a notebook. Really, it works. To be honest, that is still my favorite style of digging deeper into Scripture on a retreat. Cross-references are a nice bonus, but it is fun just to go sleuthing on your own.

But I don't do much digging in my day-to-day Bible reading. For many years I have used a daily reading plan created by The Navigators that takes me through the whole Bible in a year.[2] The beauty of the plan is covering Genesis to Revelation each year with four readings a day; the downside is that you need to move pretty fast to keep up. I make notes of points to explore more deeply, and I use my retreat times to revisit those sections. It's a great way to hone in on areas where I've heard God's voice all year long.

On my first retreat, I spent a great deal of time on the first chapter of Ephesians. I found each verse so loaded with application, it was delicious to savor for a while. Other chunks of Scripture that have been satisfying to me include the Isaiah 40s; John 14, 15, and 16; Colossians 3; Psalm 119; and many more.

Ready to try going old school with just your Bible and pen? There are two styles of getting into the Bible that you might find helpful. Don't be put off by the fancy names.

Inductive Bible Study

I learned about inductive Bible study back in college when I was part of InterVarsity Christian Fellowship. Without getting too technical, here are the three basic steps for examining a short portion of Scripture:

1. Observation: What does the verse or passage say?
2. Interpretation: What does it mean?
3. Application: How does the meaning apply to me?

Let's look at an example from Ephesians 1:18:

> I pray that the eyes of your heart may be enlightened in order that you may know the hope to which he has called you, the riches of his glorious inheritance in his holy people.

What does the verse or passage say? When our hearts are able to perceive the plan God designed for us, we can grasp more of the hope he offers. God has something really good in mind, a "glorious inheritance" to share with us.

What does it mean? God wants us in on his plans; he isn't trying to hide them, and it is okay to pray for more clarity. In fact, each of us is called to hope for all he has prepared for us.

How does the meaning apply to me? Knowing more of God's plans sounds great, and I really like the idea that I am called to receive them. I am curious about the "glorious inheritance," but it sounds exciting and wonderful. I will start praying for more.

Lectio Divina

The second method goes by the name of *lectio divina,* which is Latin for "divine reading." This method of reading the Bible has four parts, also with Latin names. I know—you might already be confused, so what's with the Latin? Just hang with me.

1. *Lectio* (read). Read the verse/passage very slowly. Notice if any word seems significant. Try to stay in the stillness of the moment.

2. *Meditatio* (meditate). Read the entire text again, holding on to the words or phrases that seem to stand out. Ponder those words. By the way, this is not the same as the meditation that is part of some Eastern religions. You don't empty your mind. Just the opposite: your goal is to fill it with the words of God.

3. *Oratio* (pray). Enter into a loving conversation with God about what you've read. Let him know your longings and concerns. Listen for how he might speak to you. You aren't likely to hear an audible voice, but what thoughts run through your mind? What life issues does the verse speak to?

4. *Contemplatio* (contemplate). Sit in silence and let God's love fill you. Enjoy the quiet, and don't hurry on.

Listening to God can come in many other forms too, but these methods should get you started.

Now let me tell you about one more retreat style you might like.

---

what other women have to say

"One night on my retreat as I lay in bed, alone and quiet, I heard his voice very clearly about a new direction he wanted me to take. When I get discouraged I remember that moment—what I heard and what it felt like—and am encouraged to press on."—Lora

"I loved the verses I meditated on from Isaiah 40 and Ephesians 1: 'He [gently] leads those that have young.' Wow. The season of life with small children is hard and God knows it and tenderly leads me. This helped me have more compassion for myself."—Darilyn

"Years ago when I was trying to make a decision on whether it was time to leave a ministry I was working for, I went on a personal retreat to pray about the decision. God spoke to me through the verses Philippians 1:9–11. God enlightened me to the truth that it wasn't about which decision was right or wrong, but which decision was best for me at the time. This really helped me to make the decision to leave the ministry with a sense of peace."—Janice

A Goal-Setting Retreat:
What's the Plan?

Goal setting is my favorite thing to do while on a retreat. Maybe it is because I am a life coach, but I swoon at the sight of a calendar and manage to maintain at least three at a time.

Crazy, but one of the paradoxes of Scripture is that we are called both to plan and then to hand the plan over to God in case he has a different agenda. Hard for a girl like me.

My most recent retreat involved lots of planning. I couldn't wait to get there with all my notebooks, calendars, and lists. Although I am a "paper" girl, I set up an electronic calendar for the first time and felt so professional. It was actually hard to sit still and pray first, committing the time and the next season to God. All I wanted to do was start filling in the blank calendar spaces.

New schedules entice me as do the fresh rhythms of each new day. Every time the calendar page turns to the next month, I want to take a turn with it to try something new. It's like New Year's Day every month. What is this month, this season, this year going to look like? Only God knows the answer, but taking some time away to ask him about it and create a rough draft is always a good exercise.

Some of us are goal setters, and I know some of you cringe at the concept. Where do you fit on the planning spectrum between spontaneity and goal setting? Do you make to-do lists for each day/month/year? Do you love to cross off items as you accomplish them?

I keep an inexpensive, five-by-eight-inch notebook with tear-off pages for my to-dos; I review it every morning and then cross off items as the day goes on. Many good systems are available for us list makers.

Maybe you like a more generalized "sometime I would like to [fill in the blank]" without getting too specific about when. A life list would fit into this category. Years ago I spent my bonus hour in October creating my own life list: those things I wanted to learn or experience in the course of the rest of my life. I keep the list handy to pray over and, of course, check off. Do you have a list like that? You could after your next retreat.

Goals have been termed "dreams with deadlines." Somehow that makes them seem friendlier, don't you think? Although I have always been a planner, I didn't really get into goal setting until I read Anne Ortlund's *Disciplines of the Beautiful Woman*. I discovered this gem a long time ago, and it still has a prominent place on my bookshelf. The author invites the reader to create life goals: "Under the wonderful umbrella of 'if God wills,' we need to decide where we suspect he wants us to go."[3] Enticing question, isn't it? I enjoy asking it at regular intervals.

Does this type of retreat interest you? If so, you've got lots of options! Check out the following goal-setting menu to see which style might be *your* style.

Life Goals

Life goals don't change from year to year but define the overall direction of your life's journey. It could be a list of four to six items of priority or a simple mission statement.

Here are mine from my first goal-setting retreat many years ago. As you can see, they are meant to last a lifetime. The older I grow in the faith as well as in years, the more I realize that God's agenda is always in the direction of what he wants me to grow into more than what he wants me to do in a day.

1. Glorify God daily in my inward and outward life.
2. Love and support my husband so he can serve God to his fullest capacity.
3. See each of our children fully following Jesus.
4. Serve the body of Christ in love and flow in the gifts God has given me.
5. Be "salt and light" to the world around me.

Five-to-Ten-Year Goals

Can you project where you would like to be in five to ten years? What would it take to get there? Some of the five-to-ten-year goal categories might include family, career, ministry, and education. Ask God to give you some direction to fill in a few blanks.

One-Year Goals

One year from now, how do you want your life to look? Your family? Your work? Your body? Dream big but be realistic. From there, plan backward. What needs to be in place in six months? Three months? Next month? Next week?

Short-Term Goals

You can choose almost anything as a short-term goal. One of my faves is "Ten Goals in Ninety Days." It is a short-term commitment, yet it's long enough to make a difference. To do this exercise, think over different areas of your life and pinpoint what actions over the course of the next ninety days would bring satisfying, realistic results. Funny how the short-term goals add up to become long-term ones. See appendix A for more details and specific questions to think through.

Of course, if you make your plans, choose your goals, and then just leave them in your retreat file, they won't serve you well or likely even be accomplished. Would you feel comfortable sharing your list with your spouse, friend, or small group? How about praying over it on a regular basis? Ask God and yourself what kind of accountability would be the most effective to ensure success.

Restorative, listening, and *planning* are just three of the retreat styles available. Don't get too caught up in picking the "right one." Each one will deliver a good outcome, so choose based on your season of life and felt need, and pick another style the next time.

Now let's look at the specifics of what you do when you arrive at your retreat.

what other women have to say

"I also get a lot out of setting goals and priorities on retreats as they align themselves with what I am discovering in prayer time. I like to come away with plans and energy for reentering the daily routine. I don't want to feel like my spiritual time is ending; I want to continue on in a fresher way, even as the daily schedule comes back."—Debbie

"On retreats, I often read through my journals from the past six months to remember where I've been and then consider where I want to focus my time and energy in the coming months."—Emery

"One of the retreat exercises was to think about and write down what my 'perfect' day would look like. Doing this helped me realize that I am already closely living my dream, and that floods me with thankfulness. It also serves as a benchmark that I can turn to when life becomes too hectic or when I need to renew my sense of purpose."—Missy

Chapter 4

THE DETAILS

Answering More of Your Questions

I know you are probably waiting for me to tell you *exactly* what to do in your time away. I've been where you are. Perhaps because I'm a firstborn who feels dutiful about following an official plan, or perhaps because I simply felt unqualified, I also wanted a preplanned program for my first retreat.

Taking a personal retreat seems a big enough step of faith without having to plan it too. I get it. For those of you who will feel more secure with a schedule in hand, I'll come back around to that.

For now, let's start with a few common questions about your actual retreat time.

What's the Deal with Silence?

"Does my retreat have to be silent?"

"Well, my friend," Letitia says with a sly grin, "that depends." I can almost hear your cry: "Noooo! Just answer the question."

For some, silence stands as the gold standard of a personal retreat. After all, that's the tradition of those who walk tight with the Lord, right? Shouldn't the absence of noise be something we strive for? It calms the soul and certainly contrasts the sound track of most of our day-to-day lives. But how essential is it? And must it be for everyone?

My first few personal retreats ended up on the silent side, not because I chose that option but because no one was around to engage in conversation. Remember, on my first retreat I arrived at breakfast and lunch to find my meals all set up, seemingly by angels, so I never exchanged a word with any of the servers.

I found it a fascinating experience to not say a word for many hours, not even a quiet "Hi." It seemed I was transported to a very different place after my initial check-in. I ran into no one. After many retreats, I can say that this doesn't always happen, but it didn't take me long that first time to immerse into the lovely sound of silence.

One year I visited a new-to-me retreat center and joined a few other ladies at a lunch table. When I first sat down, I initiated chitchat, as usual, and received some pretty pointed glares. I wondered why I was getting the silent treatment until a nun quietly pointed out the sign over the table: PLEASE OBSERVE THE COURTESY OF SILENCE DURING ALL MEALS. Oops!

Silence isn't just for personal retreats. I have also attended several group retreats that included large segments of personal silent time. During these retreats, meals were also talk-free, but one of the leaders read aloud from a spiritual classic while we dined, so it really didn't feel awkward or rude not to converse with my table mates. Of course, asking for something to be passed without speaking led to a few silent chuckles. By the second meal we managed just fine.

How would you respond to long stretches of silence? Do you think it would enhance your retreat experience? Or does the idea of not talking at all to anyone squeeze past your comfort zone? For an introverted gal like me, silence is energizing at many points in my daily life. But for you extroverts, it could be a big step. Maybe you're already looking for a way to avoid such retreats.

Here is a new angle: some retreatants make the distinction between *absolute* silence (no noise at all) and *functional* silence (no engaging in conversation but allowing music).

The absolutist camp believes God is best heard in the absence of any noise, including the noise of our own thoughts. The retreatant is urged to eliminate external sounds and avoid internal chatter. Techniques of deep breathing, relaxation techniques, and biblical meditation are often mentioned as aids to engaging in silence.

You can find more details on how to implement these practices in Ben Campbell Johnson and Paul Lang's *Time Away: A Guide for Personal Retreat*. The authors report, "Silence is like a safe haven protecting us against the noise that beats on our senses and breaks us down."[4] Those who practice this discipline have impressive testimonies about finding God in the silence. Go for it if you are enticed by the concept, but absolute silence is certainly not a mandate.

Functional silence might be a better fit for you. You avoid intentional conversation but let your smartphone music set the tone in your room or on your walks. Functional silence could also include your own singing, playing instruments, or other forms of worship. Attending an on-site service, or listening to a message or someone reading aloud, could also fit into functional silence.

How does that sound? (Excuse the pun.)

If you're still not sure about the whole silent thing, experiment with different models while you are on your retreat, including no silence at all. I can assure you, God will meet you if you show up. He is quite comfortable in any setting.

One topic to consider in the silent-or-not question is contact with the home team. Do you want to check in at home or be reachable for anything other than an emergency? Is having a quick conversation with your spouse or children at the end of the day important to you? Do you want to receive texts or emails on your phone or laptop? How about contact from work?

With today's technology, most of us are on standby all the time for anyone who wants to reach us. This competes for the focus a retreat invites and disrupts a sense of silence, whether absolute or functional. So how do you want to handle the matter? There are no rules, but it's a good idea to decide beforehand if possible.

Consider your needs before you come. Talk with those most likely to want to contact you, and set some parameters; be intentional about who has access to you. Your retreat experience will be better for it.

what other women have to say

"In the hustle and bustle of the everyday, it's hard to go really deep with God. When everything is quiet, entering into that deep place is so refreshing and reviving. The retreat experience has put me in a stronger place with my faith."—Robin

"I decided to spend Thanksgiving weekend at home one year in retreat mode: no radio, no TV, no computer, no phone, no music. Just reading some resources recommended by friends whose spirituality I admired."—Melanie

"My expectations are to settle my soul and spirit, be still, and listen. I turn off technology; I am not accessible unless there's an emergency. I invite God to come and meet with me, and he always shows up."—Lora

To Eat or Not to Eat?

Yes, another decision. I know you might not have ever considered the concept of fasting, but to eat or not to eat is a good question to consider for some retreatants.*

---

*Many books and articles are available on the practical points of entering a fast, maintaining it, and breaking it at the end. Campus Crusade for Christ (CRU) provides one of the most succinct resources I've found at https://www.cru.org/train-and-grow/spiritual-growth/fasting/7-steps-to-fasting.html.

Fasting is the practice of choosing not to eat at all or refraining from certain kinds of foods for a period of time. Fasting is a part of Jewish and Muslim holiday observances, and in various forms it has also been practiced by Christians for centuries as a spiritual discipline. Some feel that a personal retreat can be enriched by fasting. It is not for everyone; in fact, only a relative few retreatants include it as part of their retreat. But while fasting is not magical, it can do you good. Scripture provides many examples to show its spiritual benefits. Moses, Esther, King David, the prophets, Jesus, the apostles, Paul, and no doubt many other biblical characters fasted (2 Sam. 12:16; Esther 4:3; Dan. 9:3; Matt. 4:2).

If you are still shaking your head, just move on to the next section. Your retreat is valid and pleasing to Jesus if you eat and drink. But if you are curious or excited about the idea of fasting, read on.

Why would someone choose not to eat on a retreat? What are the advantages? The drawbacks?

Many feel that forgoing physical food in favor of spiritual food is rewarded by intensity in prayer, deeper communion with God, and breakthroughs for long-standing issues. If that's what you're looking for, missing a meal or two may be well worth the hunger pangs.

It might help to know that some women find it easier to fast on a retreat. The usual food triggers aren't around, nor is the distraction of preparing meals for others. Also, fasting can sap your physical energy, and it's often easier to rest on a retreat than at home.

As with silence, fasting doesn't have to be all or nothing. Partial fasts can work well on your retreat. One meal can be skipped and the time used for prayer or study instead. If you wish to start with a one-day fast, try beginning the night before by skipping dinner. Eliminating breakfast and lunch the next day and resuming food for the evening meal can be an easier way to start.

If you enjoy snacking, you could forgo treats during your retreat. You'll be amazed at what this small change will do for enhancing your focus. Letting go of coffee for the time might be another angle, if you can handle the headache.

Whether fasting benefits your retreat can depend on the type of retreat you choose. The listening retreat described in the last chapter could be enhanced by fasting. The planning retreat, on the other hand, might require mental acuity supported by regular meals. Fasting also might not fit the restorative retreat, which usually includes quality nutrition at regular intervals. Your decision whether to fast can be made closer to your actual retreat after prayerful consideration.

what other women have to say

"I have fasted a couple of times because I thought planning light, limited meals would help keep me focused and not let my mind wander."—Melanie

"Fasting helped me enter into the retreat more as I was trying to make a major life decision."—Janice

"I have never fasted on a retreat."—Robin

Is It Okay to Bring a Friend?

Some women just don't feel "ready" to go it alone and prefer to take a retreat with a friend or two. It just feels too scary or too spiritual to walk in alone. Would that describe you? You're not alone.

For many years, I retreated mostly by myself except for the time I described in the previous chapter when my friend wanted to come along. I was so eager for the time alone without my usual four companions (my kids) that I wanted it to start from the minute I left my front door. That was then; in this current season of my life, I have plenty of alone time. A friend often tags along for the fun of the drive together; then once we arrive at our retreat location, we go our separate ways.

Bringing a friend doesn't invalidate a personal retreat. It just changes the retreat from private to semiprivate. The advantages include companionship for mealtimes, taking a walk together, or just enjoying a break with each other. Friends can also pray for one another or be sounding boards for retreat discoveries. The disadvantages are letting conversations distract you, failing to get in sync with each other's break times, and interrupting your personal pacing for the retreat. You might be focused on a section of Scripture or goal setting when a knock at the door causes you to lose the moment.

It is nice to travel and eat with someone as well as have some shared downtime at the end of the day. On a recent retreat, my friend and I met at an appointed time to walk through the beautiful garden on the property, but most of the time we were on our own tracks. This won't work with every friend, so think carefully about whom you might be retreat-compatible with.

Here are a few guidelines for a tandem retreat:

· Choose a place where you can each have your own room. Of course it is usually cheaper to share a room, but is that the point?
· Talk about expectations for the time a few days before you get there and not just during the car ride. Are you each going to have separate, albeit side-by side, personal retreats? Or will you integrate your time in some way?
· Get specific about how much time you expect to spend together so both of you are on the same page. Meals? Breaks? Taking a walk together?
· Agree to pray for each other throughout the retreat, and decide if you want to start and end with prayer together.
· Choose whether you will schedule a time to share what's happening for each of you.

· Decide whether texting/phoning/knocking on the door to say hi is okay.

I encourage women to take retreats alone at least some of the time, but if starting out with a friend gets you in the door, then start there. See appendix D for ideas for a group personal retreat.

what other women have to say

"One long retreat weekend I scheduled a breakfast with good friends. We sat at the table for more than three hours, talking and laughing and telling stories. The laughter especially was healing to my soul."—Julia

"One question I asked myself on retreat was, 'Do I have a longing in my heart that I'd like to present to God as a request?' During our retreat debriefing in community (five other women I trust), naming that longing out loud and receiving prayer over it was very significant."—Ann

"Time alone and time away makes me feel refreshed, and I crave that in my busy season of life."—Julie

What Is Spiritual Direction and Do You Need It?

Don't you love all these options! Spiritual direction is an old practice, but it seems to be getting a lot of new devotees. Richard Foster defines spiritual direction as "a process through which one person helps another person understand what God is doing and saying."[5] It's sort of like working with a spiritual coach.

Many retreat centers, especially convents and monasteries, offer spiritual direction. You can arrange to meet with a trained spiritual companion at your retreat to help the process along. This person will listen to you on spiritual matters and help you reflect on your relationship with God. Your director might offer suggestions for your time, such as Scriptures to meditate on or spiritual exercises to try (such as the previously mentioned *lectio divina*).

Although spiritual direction at a retreat is usually a one-time encounter with a staff member at the facility, some women desire an ongoing relationship with a spiritual director after the retreat. A monthly meeting usually provides the same benefits.

Are you already working with a spiritual director? Your director could help you plan your retreat before you go. A clergy member at your church or an experienced believer could do the same.

Many women choose to be their own spiritual directors, so to speak. If you have a clear sense of how you want to use your retreat time and what your focus is going to be, you are probably fine without an extra layer of direction.

Are You Overwhelmed?

If you are a wing-it kind of girl, you'll plan as you go along and won't be bothered by all these details.

If you are wired more like me, you will want to know all your options so you can make some choices, at least for the *next* retreat.

Whether you talk or practice silence, eat or fast, go by yourself or bring a friend, sit down with a spiritual director or set your own direction, it is still your getaway with God, and he is waiting to meet you right where you are. Keep your focus on that fact and don't get too distracted by the details.

The next chapter will provide schedule templates for three different retreat formats. If you have been waiting for the "Just tell me what to do" section, this will be it.

what other women have to say

"I kept asking God, 'Why am I here? What am I supposed to work on?' repeatedly. Finally, I 'heard,' *Just shush and listen to me. I just wanted to see if you'd come to be with me.* Only by completely changing your environment and eliminating all distractions can you open yourself to new thoughts and interactions."—Susan

"This last retreat was harder because I felt lonely. I was processing difficult issues that were painful to ruminate on. Yet I did hear God's direction in how to pray for myself and for others. I also sensed a gentle nudging to make amends to those I had hurt. I found Scriptures to help frame the discord in my soul."—Emery

"I've often been rewarded by meeting with the spiritual directors at retreats. It helps to have a person connected to God but outside of my life to help me center and reflect. In the midst of our conversations, I see more clearly."—Mary

Chapter 5

THE SCHEDULE

Designing Your Retreat

At last, a schedule. If you're like me, you probably jumped to this chapter right away to get the details of *exactly* how to use the time. Whether you need something structured or prefer to go with the flow, look at the following schedules and details as suggested templates, a starting place to build your own timetable.

Since retreats come in all different sizes, I've provided a few sample schedules for a variety of time periods. How much time away can you take? The equivalent of a work or academic day? The time when your kids are in school? Believe me, I get that it's difficult to pull off a whole day or more from the usual script of the week. But once you start basking in the presence of God and feeling his love flowing into you, your misgivings will fade.

Sample One-Day Retreat Schedule

I realize you might need to take a vacation day or be in debt to a friend for a whole day of childcare, but if you can take a workday—approximately eight hours—then this is a perfect schedule for you.

All times I've listed below are approximate. Take more or less time as you need or feel led.

The Day Before

Get a jump start on your getaway the night before by gathering what you'll need. Like what? Pack your Bible, notebook, journal, devotional book, iPod. Don't forget the bubble bath if it fits your theme. Do you want to bring a bottle of water? How about your own lunch or snack? And don't forget comfortable shoes and clothes.

Try not to overpack. Confession: I'm guilty of this and continually attempt to bring less stuff. See the sidebar in chapter 2 on page 25 for suggestions of what to bring. Do you need to set an "away" email or record a phone message? Save time in the morning by doing as much as you can beforehand.

Retreat Day

Aim to be out the door as early as you can. Do you want to eat your breakfast at home, on the way, or when you get to your retreat destination? (Unless, of course, you are fasting.)

9:00–10:00 AM

Once you arrive and get checked in, unpack your bag and settle into your space. I like to carefully place my items around the room so it seems inviting and prepared for *me*. If it's your first time to this place, orient yourself to the parts of the facility you are in, locate the bathroom if it's down the hall, and when you are ready, settle into a comfortable chair.

Start by inviting God's presence with you to be felt and known. Commit your retreat time to the Lord for his purposes, especially if you aren't sure exactly what they are. Praying this aloud or writing it down is a helpful practice. Wait a few minutes before moving on so you can enjoy the quiet.

Next, I like to meditate on a portion of Scripture. Sometimes I know ahead of time what passage it is; other times God leads me somewhere in the Bible. I usually pick a passage different from my daily Bible reading guide just to mix it up. Stay with this for about twenty minutes.

Need some direction? Check out Psalm 18, Romans 12, Ephesians 1, or John 15. Just pick one, though. Take your time—these are loaded passages.

Can't stop the flow of to-dos racing through your mind? This is common when you first enter into retreat. Take a few moments to do the "On My Mind" exercise described in appendix A.

10:00 AM–Noon

Now that you are settled in and have dedicated your day to God, spent some time in the Word, and harnessed the distractions, let's move into the theme of your retreat as we discussed in chapter 3.

If you are on a *restorative retreat*, take a morning stroll to find some beauty in nature. See what signs of God you can find on your walk. Develop a practice of moving *slowly* throughout the time. Walk slowly, respond slowly, and eat slowly. Settle into his pace for you to rest.

If you came to *listen* to God through his Word, pull out your tools. Did you bring a Bible study along? Time to jump in. Did you plan to do an inductive Bible study or *lectio divina*? Try to get one segment in now. Are you digging deep into a biblical theme? Start with your print concordance or an Internet resource on your phone or computer, such as BibleGateway.com, to see what pops up. (Yes, I know it can be overwhelming to see all the options.)

Maybe you want to study a biblical character. Did you choose someone well known or more obscure? Why do you think you were drawn to this person? How would you like to approach the study? List their character traits? Place yourself in the story? Reflect on what it would be like to be friends with this individual? Google your person to see what comes up (or not if you don't trust yourself not to get lost online).

Are you taking a *planning retreat*? Use this morning time to review all the components of your life, as though you are cleaning out your purse, and ask God how he would like to rearrange each item. As David wrote in Psalm 5:3, "Every morning I lay out the pieces of my life on your altar and watch for fire to descend" (MSG). Don't expect lightning to fall from the sky, as God so often works in quiet ways, but trust that you've been heard. You may not receive definitive answers right away—although you might—but you can at least start the process.

Thinking about new short-term goals? Can you get a rough draft done before lunch? I like to start with all the possibilities and narrow them down to the ones God seems to highlight. You'll have time to refine them in the afternoon.

If you have a little time before lunch, take another walk.

Noon–1:00 PM

Time for a break to eat the lunch you brought, stroll to the dining room of the retreat facility, or pick up something nearby. If you are fasting, still stop for a break and use this time for concentrated prayer. The lunch break can also include a walk around the facility. Visit the chapel or bookstore, if they have one. No need to rush for once.

1:00–1:30 PM

If you are sleepy, this is a good time for a short nap. You might want to set your phone alarm so the afternoon doesn't get away—though if you are on a restorative retreat, snooze to your heart's content.

1:30–3:30 PM

Ready to get back into your primary agenda?

If you're a *restoration* seeker, then once you wake up from your long nap, you can look for other ways to be refreshed. Is there art on display that you can view at the retreat center? Did you bring some music to enjoy? Maybe you packed a beautiful picture book to indulge in. Use this time to allow yourself to unwind.

If you came to focus on *listening* to God through his Word, single out another portion of Scripture to study, or pick up where you left off in your biblical theme or character study. But don't be surprised if God leads you in a different direction than you intended when you started. God is like that. Since he has your attention, he might have some new things to show you in his Word.

If you are primarily *planning*, get specific by using the SMART goal model: specific, measurable, attainable, realistic, time-bound. Just saying "eat healthier" is way too vague. Try "count my fruits and vegetables each day." If by nature you are a planner, start blending all your great ideas with your calendar and family schedule to see what can actually work in this season. Make a list of what needs to be decided, consulted, or purchased. Need to make a medical appointment? Plan a baby shower? Talk to your sister about your mom's vision issues? See how these items fit on your actual calendar.

3:30–4:00 PM

This is a good time for an afternoon break. If you haven't ventured outdoors for a longer walk, do it now, even if it is not perfect weather. Resist the notion to check emails or voicemails except for an emergency. I like to prepare a cup of tea to relax with and enjoy; usually I bring my own in case my favorite flavor isn't available from the common snack area.

4:00–4:45 PM

Begin to wrap up your day. Finish any Bible studies you may have started. Recopy your goals and pray over them. Take a look at the calendar you created and commit your time slots to God. Enjoy this last bit of rest.

4:45–5:00 PM

Take your time packing up your stuff, then go back to the chair where you started the day. Ask for God's help in your reentry, safety in getting home, and help in retaining the take-aways of the day.

Make sure you leave your space cleared as requested. Check out at the desk if required, and then head home.

What if you feel like you didn't hear much or aren't sure what the results were from the day? Some of my retreats have felt like that. It was only later that I saw the fruit from the time away, and it wasn't always what I expected. When we give the time to God, it is his to do with as he pleases, but be assured, he will use that time you've offered to him.

Sample Overnight Retreat Schedule

Can you get away overnight? Having twenty-four hours can provide unexpected and delightful possibilities.

Day 1
If You Arrive Before Dinner

Unpack and take a short walk to get acquainted with the facility. If there is enough time, settle in and pray for your retreat or read a short portion of Scripture, such as the chapter of Proverbs that corresponds to the day (for example, read Proverbs 21 on the twenty-first day of the month) or a few psalms. It takes some transition time to separate from the day's events.

Dinner

Savor the meal and eat without rushing. Might be a change, right? Thank God for each person involved in getting the food to your plate, such as the farmers, packers, truck drivers, delivery persons, cooks, and servers.

If You Arrive After Dinner
Settle in as described above, then pick up the schedule here.

After Dinner
Return to your room, get comfortable, and ask God what is on his mind for your time away. Sometimes it helps to imagine you are chatting with Jesus and getting a checkup, just as you would at the doctor's office. Let him know how your body feels, what's filling your mind, your concerns about the health of your family, and anything else that bubbles up.

Target your prayers on your time at the retreat, the people you've left behind, and other concerns God lays on your heart. Pull out your journal and write down your intentions for the retreat.

If you still have energy, consider an interesting exercise I call "look back," in which you review your last few months or more. What were dominant themes? There are seasons when health issues, work deadlines, or home renovations seem to define every day.

What surprised you? Often it is not until we take a good look back that we can see all the fears and anxieties of our last few months. Was God speaking to you about a particular theme such as gratitude or serving? Stay with this for a while.

This might be all you can process the first night. Sometimes it seems as though the whole point of the "night before" is just to get you at the location for a fresh start in the morning. It's really fine not to accomplish much in the evening. Showing up counts a lot.

If you are a night owl, you might want to add a few other activities. If you're at a retreat center, take a walk to the chapel and envision Jesus sitting on the seat next to you. If you feel stuck, sing a worship song or read aloud from Psalms in your room. Have you ever prayed the "Order of Compline" from the Book of Common Prayer?[6] This is an ancient prayer for the end of the day.

As soon as you feel sleepy, slowly get ready for bed and start your rest. You might include some light reading or music to help you unwind. Instead of counting sheep (does anybody really do this?), I sometimes pray for every person who ever slept in my room. I don't know their names, but God does.

Day 2

Up early? Just lingering in bed can be a delicious, rare option. If you like to get going and usually practice a morning prayer ritual, start with that. Maybe you'd like to stretch or listen to music. If corporate prayer sounds interesting, many retreat centers offer morning devotions that are open to retreatants. You can always take a short walk or run if you're an active-in-the-morning girl. Or just slide into breakfast if that's your morning style.

After breakfast, pick up the eight-hour retreat schedule I outlined earlier in this chapter.

Sample Weekend Retreat Schedule

Ah, the luxury of a whole weekend getaway with God!

A full weekend will incorporate the same components of a shorter retreat but with longer chunks of time to savor the moments and dig deeper into restoring, listening, or planning.

Friday Night

For this longer model, you can spend more time on the first day enjoying God's presence before you enter into your agenda. Consider adding some worship time on the front end of your retreat.

If worship outside of church is new to you, start with listening to worship music on your smartphone or laptop. I have a couple of Pandora stations for what I call "holy music," which set the tone. Add your own voice to the melody and direct your singing to God. If you don't have a way to play music, sing some familiar tunes. (Christmas carols count too!) Perhaps there is a hymnal on the premises you can use.

While in your room, if you're comfortable with dancing as a way of worship, dance along with the music. No one is watching except the One to whom you dance.

Follow the first evening's agenda in the twenty-four-hour retreat, described earlier in this chapter.

Saturday

Morning

Such a delight to wake up in a new place! You might want to begin as with the other models in this chapter, but you have the luxury of the extra time to go deeper with the exercises.

When you are ready to move into the retreat practices of the day, allow about an hour for prayer as the first exercise. "An hour!" you might gasp. Yes, it's more doable than you may realize. Here are a few ways to spend the time:

- Visualize your individual family members and hold them up to God, asking for his blessing on them. Focus on how thankful you are for each person rather than concentrating on your fix-it list for them. I use photos of my family when I pray for them, and I have created a section in my prayer journal that combines their photos and their prayer needs. See appendix B on "How I Changed My Picture of Prayer."
- Give thanks for each part of your body, even the parts that aren't working so well. Thank God that you have the physical strength to come on this retreat. As a hospital chaplain, I realize how grateful I am for things I used to take for granted, such as legs and feet to keep walking, eyes to see this page, ears to hear music, a voice to sing and pray. Keep going.
- Do you have a job? Give thanks for your employment and the people you work for and with. If you are a caregiver for your children or parents, thank God for the opportunity to serve them.

- Thank God for your neighbors, extended family, and church community. Even if you don't know your neighbors, you can still pray for the "family in the blue house, the single gal in the apartment upstairs, and the couple on the corner lot." Picture yourself pouring blessing down on each one with your prayers. Maybe you are the only one praying right this moment for your church, community, and family.
- Spend time giving thanks for your finances, health, or anything else troubling you. Okay, that could be loaded, but start with thanks.
- Use the ACTS model of prayer: adoration (worship), confession (never a lack in that department for me), thanksgiving, and supplication (a fancy word for asking). I'm sure you have a mental list handy for what you need and want.

Remember, you are just having a conversation with Jesus. No one is grading your prayers.

When you're done praying, sit quietly. Do you feel God's presence? Hear him speak into your heart? What do you think he is saying? Write it down in your journal, even if you are unsure. Years ago a friend showed me how she uses a different color ink in her journal when she writes what she thinks God is speaking. I decided to try that too, and now I use purple ink for God interspersed with my own blue thoughts.

After your hour is complete, go ahead and pull out your Bible. Are you following a reading guide or Bible study? Dig in just as you would if you were home. Expect the verses to be more illumined in this setting because you aren't rushing off to the next thing.

After your prayer and reading, turn to the purpose of your retreat. If you came for *restoration*, consider adding a beauty treatment at this point, à la Queen Esther's rounds of beauty treatments (see Esther 2). You won't have twelve months, but how about twelve minutes? Did you bring oils or lotion along? Spend time carefully applying them as you thank God for your skin. Simple stretching can feel so good too.

Did you come to *listen*? You might want to start with just sitting for a few minutes and simply notice your breathing. Have you heard of the Jesus Prayer? Very simple: "Lord Jesus Christ, son of David, have mercy on me." You breathe in: "Lord Jesus Christ, son of David." Breathe out: "Have mercy on me." It might feel strange at first, so don't worry. Sometimes I meditate on a name of God during each inhale and exhale. He has a *lot* of names: Immanuel, Counselor, Savior, Mighty God, Rock, Deliverer, to list a few.

Select a portion of Scripture to study unhurriedly. Earlier in chapter 3, I explained a couple of methods for deeper Bible study, such as inductive and *lectio divina*. Have you ever delved into John 14? This is a great chapter to use for a deeper study as it centers on Jesus's desire to be with us forever. Some of my other "greatest hits" of the Bible are Isaiah 43, 2 Timothy, and Colossians 3 because they seem to always tell me what I need to hear in the moment.

As you study each verse, listen for the Holy Spirit to speak to you about what you are reading. Does any of this apply to your life right now? Most likely, yes.

Try interspersing your chosen Scriptures with a psalm, and pray it to God. With 150 psalms to choose from, I'm sure you'll find one that fits. Just scroll through a few until you find some you connect with. Feeling adventurous? Experiment with singing the psalm and make up the melody. This is not *American Idol*, so let go and give it all you've got. Your audience of One will be silently cheering.

Is your retreat purpose to do some *planning*? With a whole day, you should be able to make a lot of progress. When else are you going to have this kind of time? If you want to take a long-range look, consider Michael Hyatt and Daniel Harkavy's life-planning tools.[7] Check out chapters 11, 12, and 13 in the next section for more ideas on how to use one day for life review.

Stop for lunch and set the work aside. Eat in silence, and try to be fully aware of your surroundings.

Afternoon

After lunch take a nap to refresh yourself for the rest of the day. How long you snooze depends on your retreat's theme or your current need. Do you need just a quick recharge or a deep drink of rest? Only you can answer that, girlfriend. Once you're awake, stretch a bit. Head outdoors and take a longer walk. Use as many of your senses as you can, and enjoy your own pace.

When you return, pick up where you left off, and continue for the next hour or so. By now, it is probably late afternoon. Stop for a cup of tea or another beverage.

At this point you might feel finished with your primary agenda. You got away, you spent time with God, you followed direction, and you are ready to stick with a light schedule the rest of the time. Go for it, girl—well done. You might opt to take another walk or pick up a devotional book or other light reading to fill the time until dinner.

On the other hand, you might be one of those gals who pick up steam as the day goes on. Go with the flow of your energy level. I'm more the "wind down as the day passes" type, so I don't usually target activities involving a lot of concentration after mid-afternoon. You know how you're wired; trust the flow.

Evening

After dinner, once again follow how you sense God leading. I recommend taking about an hour to review and wrap up the day, then relax with a book or a bath until you are ready for an early bedtime.

Sunday

Most venues have a late-morning checkout time, so your focus is likely on getting packed to head home sometime after breakfast.

Have some time available? Consider stopping off at an unfamiliar church for the Sunday morning service. Without the familiar props and people, you might experience God in a new way.

Before your to-do list for the following week takes over your thoughts, spend a bit of time deciding how to hang on to the retreat experience when "normal" life resumes.

Here are a few ideas I have found to be helpful:

- Write out your takeaway points from your listening or planning or anything else in which God spoke to you.
- Keep this list someplace where you will see it: your journal, purse, phone, even your bathroom mirror. Pray over it often.
- Seek out accountability, if you created action steps. Can you ask a friend, spouse, coach, or small group to check in with you about your follow-through?
- Decide when your next retreat will be and jot it down in your calendar. Don't worry if it's not an exact date. Noting "Retreat in the fall" is good enough for now.

Whichever retreat length you choose—whether a day retreat, an overnight, or a whole weekend—start with quiet time with Jesus, then dive into your purpose. Also, be sure to spend a bit of time before leaving to determine how you'll implement the things you've learned.

Now that you've seen how doable a shorter retreat is, how does a five-day getaway sound? Tune in to part 2 for more details. But first let's look at some considerations that apply to retreats of any length.

what other women have to say

"I never use a schedule. Going with the flow is something I can only do on a retreat."—Susan

"I've been on guided personal retreats and that's been helpful, but sometimes I like unstructured time to do what the Spirit is leading me to."—Janice

"I think it helps to have structure for the retreat, but not so much that it hampers what the Holy Spirit might be doing."—Robin

Chapter 6

"BUT WAIT . . . !"

Addressing Common Concerns

I hope that by now you are at least considering that at some point you might like to have your own getaway with God. Before delving into part 2, which covers the longer retreat, let's address some concerns that might be rolling around in your head.

Concern #1:
I Have a Few Fears

When it comes to taking a retreat, fear of the unknown can pop up right at the start. You've never done anything like this before. Riding on its back might be the fear of being alone. Maybe you cannot imagine time with just you and Jesus. You are used to being around other people whom you can turn and talk to at any moment. Or perhaps you really are afraid of being all by yourself somewhere. What if there is an emergency? (I can't assure you that you won't be alone; however, others are always in reach even if you take a wilderness retreat.)

God knew we would all struggle with fear from time to time. The Bible is filled with "Do not be afraid" verses. Have you noticed them?

I think I have them all underlined in my Bible. Deuteronomy 31:8 is good for a retreat: "The LORD himself goes before you and will be with you; he will never leave you nor forsake you. Do not be afraid; do not be discouraged."

Picture yourself handing your fear over and receiving faith in return. Actually go through the motions if it helps: hold up your fear in your hands; turn your hands over, dropping the fear into God's hands; then turn your hands back up and receive faith from God in exchange.

Concern #2:
I'm Not Sure I Will Get Anything Out of It

You may think, *What if I go to all this trouble and nothing happens?* You might have had similar feelings about other important events in your life. We sometimes wonder if an occasion or trip will live up to our expectations. Feeling doubtful is a normal response to something new.

I don't know of any woman who has experienced a getaway with God where nothing happened. Something will happen, even if afterward you aren't sure what it was (unlikely) or can't quite define it. In Matthew 7:7–8, Jesus promises us, "Ask and it will be given to you; seek and you will find; knock and the door will be opened to you. For everyone who asks receives; the one who seeks finds; and to the one who knocks, the door will be opened." Count on that.

Concern #3:
I Can't Afford the Time or Money It Will Cost

For many women, issues with time or money too often cancel the whole idea of a getaway before any serious consideration goes into it. I get that, as you will see in my story in the next section. I do, however, hold to the belief that we find time and resources for what we truly want, as evidenced by the way we manage to watch our favorite

TV shows, browse online shopping, buy our favorite coffee drinks, or spend endless hours on social media. As your desire for retreat increases, the time and the means will appear.

This may sound simplistic but it has worked over and over again for me. Trust God for the resources you need. Ask him to provide. My whole five-day retreat came out of a prayer like that.

Shifting your approach from an "expense" outlook to an "investment" one can help you take the plunge. From both the time and money angles, this regular investment in getting alone with God will provide dividends to live on the rest of your life.

Concern #4:
My Family Doesn't "Get It"

This concern is a real heart tugger. It can be difficult to get your husband's blessing, especially if you're not quite sure about a retreat yourself. I encourage you to start with a short retreat, and think of the refreshed and revived wife and mom they'll receive afterward. Isn't that a great tradeoff for everyone? Can you take about the same amount of time as you would to visit an old friend or a day at the mall? Try a getaway in which your absence affects your family only minimally.

Perhaps a Saturday or Sunday would work best for you. Is there something with a similar time commitment your husband would like to do, so you can trade time away? Do you have a girlfriend with whom you could exchange kid care for a day? Ask God for a good solution, and expect it to show up.

Concern #5:
I'll Be Bored/I've Never Taken Time for Myself

You would likely be bored if you did nothing the whole time you were gone, but I don't think that is your plan, is it? The previous chapters have offered you a multitude of ideas for planning your time, and more are coming in the next section. You will have plenty to do. Most of us have a running list, at least in our heads, of what we would like to do given a few free moments. I pull out my list every year at the end of October or beginning of November, when we turn back our clocks and get a bonus hour.

I provided ideas for restoration, listening, and planning retreats, and I bet you have your own ideas for pleasurable pursuits that could fit into those frameworks. Don't plan too much, though; leave some margin. Sometimes the best times come when we don't have an exact plan, just a boatload of expectation for how God might show up. Leave room for the Holy Spirit to surprise you.

Girlfriend, I hope I have allayed some of your anxieties. Confession: I'm sometimes not one-hundred-percent certain about even my most important decisions when I make them. In the end, you might need to take a leap of faith.

what other women have to say

"You don't know what you don't know. Try it just once—you'll see. Even if you don't think you have 'something' to work on, give it a try."—Susan

"Take time to breathe . . . and let God show you who you really are: his beloved daughter."—Melanie

"When you make the commitment that God is the most important person in your life or event on your calendar, and you let nothing else intrude on your space and time with him, well, it's special."—Lora

"Taking a retreat requires courage and a sacrifice of time, but the benefits far surpass the cost."—Ann

"The world won't tell you this, but caring for your soul is the most important thing you can do. It's not only important for you, but for everyone you love."—Debbie

"I was surprised at how much Jesus was present, how much he had to say to me, and the impact this time had on life-changing decisions I made not long after."—Alison

"I've learned to move into retreat time openhanded. The mountain does not always quake and the bush doesn't always burn. When I had the expectation that something 'big' would happen, I could leave disappointed—afraid that God didn't show up. I go on retreat with the intent to rest and to listen. I let God call the shots, free of expectations."—Brenda

Chapter 7

SABBATH

Getting Away Without Going Away

Many of my stories are in these pages. I wanted to be vulnerable, hoping from my own life experiences to show you how much God loves *you*. He not only knows but cares deeply about all the details of your life.

I hope your wheels are turning toward planning your own getaway with God—or at least, that your heart is inclining that way. It may not be possible for you to leave right now, though, and most of us can't leave our homes every week anyway.

So where's a girl to go to get away more regularly? Good news: God knows exactly where you are, and he has a plan for you. There is an opportunity always waiting for you to enter into intimacy and rest without even leaving your home.

Way back in the Old Testament, God laid out a means of stepping back and being still right in the midst of a busy life. It works for everyone, even those who never take a personal retreat. You will probably recognize this plan; it has been around since Moses. I think I originally heard it mentioned in the first movie I ever saw:

Cecil de Mille's epic, *The Ten Commandments*. Have you guessed it? It's the fourth commandment: "Remember the Sabbath day by keeping it holy" (Exod. 20:8). In his infinite wisdom, God knew we would need rest but might not take it, so he included it in his top ten rules of life.

The Sabbath instruction is probably the most ignored commandment. It is easy to dismiss as "cultural" or so subject to interpretation that we miss it altogether. Yet creating a rhythm for remembering the Sabbath can result in a mini retreat every week in your own home or nearby.

Pause here for a moment and consider.

Sabbath.

How do you feel just reading that word? Enticed? Intrigued? Confused? Perhaps, "Oh no, not another thing to do." Yes, I felt that too when I first explored the Sabbath commandment. Stay with me here. I want to invite you, not drag you in.

Too often we confuse Sabbath keeping with church attending. So before you remind me that you already go to church every week, let me assure you that Sabbath is about much more than a church service. Actually, "church" isn't even mentioned in the commandment. I like the way Lynne Baab defines the practice in her book *Sabbath Keeping*: "[Sabbath is a] weekly day of rest and worship. A day to cease working and relax in God's care for us. A day to stop the things that occupy our workdays and participate in activities that nurture peace, worship, relationships, celebration and thankfulness."[8]

Doesn't that sound like a mini retreat?

Past generations seemed to have a better handle on this practice. If you ask your grandparents or older-than-your-parents friends, you might hear stories of Sabbath keeping that seemed more cultural than religious. Most folks observed the Sabbath in some way.

Growing up in a small Midwest town, I have clear memories of the clacking tongues, including my mom's, when our neighbor dared to hang out her wash on warm Sunday afternoons. "Surely she could find another time to do this" was the word on the street.

Everyone knew that Sundays were not for laundry but for church and for big dinners with extended family followed by "Sunday drives." Looking back, it doesn't sound like much of a Sabbath for the moms who prepared the feasts, but my brothers and I have fond memories of driving to watch cows get milked at the local country dairy, visiting the closest state park, and walking through historic Nauvoo, Illinois.

My husband and I also remember traveling on the East Coast in the 1970s shortly after we were married. Back then it was hard to find any stores open on Sundays, except drugstores, because of the Blue Laws. These laws were instituted in 1617 to help people "remember the Sabbath." Although most of these statutes have been repealed, many states still prohibit car sales on Sundays, which is a leftover from that era.

Let's go back even further. Have you noticed the strong sense of rhythm in God's creation? Read through the first chapter of Genesis again, starting with verse 3 ("Let there be light") and going to verse 26 ("Let us make mankind in our image"). Notice the order of events. Chapter 1 ends, "And there was evening, and there was morning—the sixth day." The Hebrew day still starts with sunset and the evening. That's why the Sabbath and all the Jewish holidays begin at night.

Besides the flow of the week—six days of work followed by one day of rest—each season held a rhythm of holy days and festivals. Some are major holidays, such as Passover; others are considered minor, such as Purim; but all provide a structure to help the Jewish people— and you, if you choose—stop and remember, rejoice, and celebrate.

The calendar on your kitchen wall also provides a rhythm of special days and ordinary days, and we need the flow of both. We long for the festivities of the holidays, then welcome the return of routine. Think of the flow and the buildup toward Thanksgiving and

Christmas, then the return to ordinary life, interspersed by Valentine's Day, St. Patrick's Day, and other minor holidays.

In the church calendar, the long liturgical season of Lent builds up to the festivities of Easter, then slides back into what are actually called "ordinary days." Then the cycle starts again with the season of Advent. Seems like we have lost that sense of rhythm with our 24/7 mentality of always being "on."

I believe "remembering the Sabbath" is still God's best plan for us—six days of work followed by a day of rest which fills us up for the new workweek. When we think we can't do another day, it's time for the rest day again.

According to Wayne Muller in *Sabbath: Finding Rest, Renewal, and Delight in Our Busy Lives*, "In the relentless busyness of modern life, we have lost the rhythm between work and rest. While many of us are tremendously weary, we have come to associate tremendous guilt and shame with taking time to rest. Sabbath gives us permission; it commands us to stop."[9]

So how does a busy, tightly scheduled woman of the twenty-first century pull this off? By first making the choice to do so and then finding a model that works for each season of her life.

However you choose to practice Sabbath, the point is to slow down with Jesus and find those things that refuel you. Jesus was all over the Pharisees for getting too literal about keeping the Sabbath, and that is not my intent. The purpose of the day is to rest from work, and that isn't just you resting—it's everyone resting. This is how it goes:

> Remember the Sabbath day by keeping it holy. Six days you shall labor and do all your work, but the seventh day is a sabbath to the LORD your God. On it you shall not do any work, neither you, nor your son or daughter, nor your male or female servant, nor your animals, nor any foreigner residing in your towns. For in six days the LORD made the heavens

and the earth, the sea, and all that is in them, but he rested on the seventh day. Therefore the LORD blessed the Sabbath day and made it holy. (Exod. 20:8–11)

You might still be wondering, What's the point? You haven't heard any sermons about this concept, and frankly, you don't want to add one more thing to your life, even if it is restful. I had the same reservations at first. Then I started gradually wading into the practice.

After a particularly stressful season when I felt totally wrung out, like a twisted towel on the bathroom floor, I heard about Karen Burton Mains's book *Making Sunday Special*.[10] The book promised inspiration and ideas on organizing the week around a day of rest. These were the pre-Amazon days when you had to order a book from a store and wait more than a week for it to come in. Before I even received the book, I was intrigued by the title and kept thinking about the notion of setting aside a day. I wasn't calling it a "Sabbath" back then, but it was the same concept.

Funny, but the first thing my husband and I did to start setting aside the day was to make waffles before church for our Sunday breakfasts. My husband made them from a simple recipe, and all of a sudden Sundays felt special. From there we agreed to decline invitations that seemed less than restful, and we began to reshape the whole day toward filling up our spirits rather than using it as an opportunity to get more done. Believe me, our Sabbaths had a lot of starts and stops at first, but eventually they evolved into the best day of the week.

After a few months of working out the details, which remain somewhat fluid each week to avoid getting legalistic about what or what not to do, the impact of our day of rest seemed to permeate well into midweek. By about Wednesday, when the pace of life seemed to ramp up, the thought of just a few more days until the next Sabbath felt like a cool breeze on a hot day.

One more thing: We can feel the benefits of that day in our relationship with Jesus too. Just as a really good time with someone we love can fill us up for days, hanging with Jesus in those Sabbath hours has a big spillover effect on the rest of our lives. Also, when we're at rest, we hear him better, and we more easily access the peace he is always trying to hand us.

But What About . . . ?

I'm sure you have questions. So here are some common ones, along with practical answers.

Can You Give Me Some Examples?

In this empty-nest season of my life, observing Sabbath starts with choosing to change the pace. After coming home from church on Sunday, I usually do very little. As an introvert, I gravitate toward quietness as a way of getting restored.

What does that mean? I schedule very few social events, avoid housework (other than cleaning up after myself), certainly schedule no meetings, and mostly stay off the phone and the computer for anything that's work related.

Instead I enjoy a longer prayer time and exchange my Monday–Saturday readings for some Sunday-only selections, such as reading all the additional Scriptures suggested in my current devotional. During the afternoon I might read the newspapers from the week (since they are always piled up), take a nap or a walk or both, read something fun, and watch TV in the evening with my husband over a simple bowl of soup. Easy and satisfying and something I can do because I have no kids around.

What If I'm an Extrovert?

For you, practicing Sabbath might include getting together with life-giving friends. Do you enjoy inviting others to your home? Trying new restaurants? Exploring local attractions without minding how many other people are there? Nothing in the concept of Sabbath implies being alone. But do look for the component of rest and staying close to Jesus for the agenda of the day.

Is There "Work" Other Than My Job?

Does Sabbath include no food preparation? No shopping? No gardening? It again depends on your definition of restful. One size does not fit all. Most moms can't get away with doing no work on Sunday. For instance, telling your kids you aren't cooking might not go over well. But that is how Orthodox Jewish women do it: they handle all the cooking the day before. You could do the same, so all you have to do on the Sabbath is warm things up. The important thing is to communicate to your family that the Sabbath day is different from the other days—and it is a good thing.

What Was That About Cooking?

Did I mention that I am not crazy about cooking? So for me to make a big meal would not be restful in the slightest. I usually prepare a "Sunday soup" in a slow cooker so I don't have to tend to it. We eat it with a salad and bread. On the other hand, one of my friends loves to cook—it fills her with energy and joy—so preparing a Sabbath meal would likely be restful for her and would fit well into her personal plan.

The same principle applies for other hobbies, such as gardening. Never a restful task for me, but it might just be the activity that draws you into the presence of God. As someone pointed out to me, an activity can be considered rest or work depending on who's doing it.

What If My Job Requires Me to Work on Sunday?

My family is full of hospital workers, so this is a common question. The instruction is to keep a *Sabbath*, not a *Sunday*. Can you find another time during the week? A "floating" Sabbath isn't ideal, but it can work.

You may be tempted to consider a "partial Sabbath," in which you grab a few hours when you can. While that might work occasionally, the intention is to include a whole day. It's hard sometimes, I know, but don't give up too soon. Ask God to show you where the rest is he has planned for you. And trust that if he commanded it, he can certainly help you take it—all of it.

How Can I Involve the Rest of My Household?

If you are in a shared household, then husband, children, other family members, or roommates are part of your day also. So how does practicing Sabbath together work out? The answer is: with a few conversations along the way and quite a few tweaks.

For many families, Sabbath is an opportunity to connect. For family members who commonly go their own ways during the week, what a great way to grow closer, relax, and enjoy time together! Here are some ideas that might help you plan:

- Play games together at home. Watching a movie can work too, but it is not as interactive.
- Parents can take turns "on duty," one spending time with the kids while the other enjoys time alone to refill and restore. Single parents can do the same with a friend.
- Read aloud to your family on Sunday nights (or whichever night is your Sabbath). My husband and I read through the whole Little House and Narnia series while we munched on countless bowls of popcorn and sliced apples.
- Store a collection of crafts/activities for Sabbath-only use. Make sure they're fun.
- Carefully look at Sunday schedules before signing your kids up for something. Sometimes it is hard to avoid schedule conflicts,

especially with team sports. Some families just say no to all Sunday commitments; others want to keep the activity but not let it take over. It can be a hard decision. Pray and ask God to lead you.

· If you are at the soccer game or other activity, practice full engagement and watch the game without reading the paper or catching up on email. This might seem like a no-brainer, but look around at the next game and see all the non-watching going on. Not multitasking for a change can be restful.

When I was a girl, Sunday nights were my family's favorite night of the week. After a large family dinner at noon, my mom took a break from cooking and we got to eat TV dinners. Remember those? My brothers and I thought they were the best ever. We actually did eat them from those aluminum trays they came in while we watched TV. *The Ed Sullivan Show* and *Bonanza* were our favorite shows, and watching them felt restful.

Some of my single girlfriends gather with close friends for a special time to share a Sabbath meal. Sometimes they do potluck, other times they order out, but the gathering is almost always held at someone's home rather than a restaurant.

Do I Need to Silence My Cell Phone?

I don't know, do you? For some, turning off the phone for at least part of the day is the most important component of Sabbath practice. It goes back to the intention of choosing rest over work. The same principle goes for checking email, surfing the Internet, and playing digital games.

What Are Some Other Sabbath Practices?

In many Jewish households, a candle might burn for the whole Sabbath. An alternative is to keep a small night light burning to remind you that you are in a different time zone. Sometimes I use an electric or flameless candle.

Some women like to wear a piece of favorite jewelry during the Sabbath. Others choose an item of Sabbath-only comfortable clothing to remind them that this day is different.

Sabbath often includes taking a nap, and in some circles, married couples are encouraged to make love on the Sabbath. The common theme here is to rest and enjoy the day.

Can you be on the lookout for beauty in nature? Try taking a walk alone or with your family, regardless of the season, to see what shows up in creation this week.

Maybe you like to listen to background music. Choose music that evokes rest and quiet to play in at least part of your home. I have a few Pandora stations that are perfect for these days.

Since this is merely a chapter, not a book, on Sabbath, I encourage you to more fully explore the concept through one of the many books available on this topic. I list a few in the sidebar below.

---

additional Sabbath resources

Still have questions? These are some of the many excellent resources out there that I would recommend:

- Wayne Muller, *Sabbath: Finding Rest, Renewal, and Delight in Our Busy Lives*
- Keri Wyatt Kent, *Rest: Living in Sabbath Simplicity*
- Marva J. Dawn, *Keeping the Sabbath Wholly: Ceasing, Resting, Embracing, Feasting*
- Lynne M. Baab, *Sabbath Keeping: Finding Freedom in the Rhythms of Rest*
- Karen Burton Mains, *Making Sunday Special* (Creative ways, new and old, to make Sunday your best day of the week)

How to Define What Is Restful

Sabbath is a gift to help you reconnect with God and to refuel. And it bears repeating that what "reconnect and refuel" looks like for me won't necessarily look the same for you. That's okay. In Mark 2:27, Jesus reminded his followers that "the Sabbath was made for man, not man for the Sabbath."

But what if you still aren't sure how you want to practice it? I may have something helpful for you.

When I started offering workshops about Sabbath, I designed a few questions for women like me who need everything spelled out. These questions help shape their Sabbath planning and participation. Your answers might help you sort out whether or not an activity fits the spirit of the Sabbath.

1. Is the activity life-giving? Does it add to my sense of balance and order? Does it center me in Christ? In the *abundant life*?
2. Can the activity be simplified? Is there an easier way to accomplish it? (Good question to ask about food preparation.)
3. Is there an alternative day or time this could be done? Can I make that phone call later in the week? Run by the store another time? Find that document on Monday?
4. Where can I find delight in the moments of the day? How can I keep a single focus instead of spinning out into multitasking?
5. How am I inviting God's presence and blessing in my plans for the day?

When I began seriously to answer those questions, I found that my entire thinking about the ways I approached and practiced Sabbath changed. Life became clearer, and I found that throughout my Sabbath—and even into the rest of the week—I felt energized to engage life more fully. I hope you have the same results.

what other women have to say

"After church I listen to worship music on Christian radio. I might do some cooking or light cleaning, but I will not do anything that makes any noise to interfere with the radio. It totally feels like a mini retreat. This time allows me to introspect on my walk with Christ and pray for whatever. I finish out the day refreshed from the last week and spiritually ready to head into the next week."—Robin

"I practice Sabbath time by relinquishing my use of electronics. Those days become free and refreshing, without the pull to check email or Facebook."—Missy

"I have a few 'rules of Sabbath' that I generally follow, but they are not set in stone, especially because I have young children. No big cooking, unless I do it in an experimental/creative way. We almost always eat hot dogs for lunch. I try to complete errands on Saturdays so I don't have to shop on Sundays. I like to do something on the Sabbath that I don't normally get to do, like reading or writing for pleasure. I also don't schedule lots of social events. Sometimes we have an event that we go to (besides church), but we try to keep those days open if we can, and we almost certainly would not do more than one. Those restorative, slow Sabbath rhythms are a gift to me and my whole family."—Ann

"I try to play more on the Sabbath."—Emery

"Life has seasons. Sabbath-keeping is a spiritual practice that has some flexibility. The outward practice must be shaped by the inward reality of your relationship with God, but it's also shaped by your circumstances."—Keri Wyatt Kent, from *Rest*[11]

"To have cocoa for breakfast instead of tea . . . to enjoy one's favorite foods only on Sunday, even to use especially precious bowls or mugs—these are a few simple examples of intentional ways to mark the Sabbath as a time for feasting, as a day of delight."—Marva J. Dawn, from *Keeping the Sabbath Wholly*[12]

"Sabbath . . . a delightful space on the weekly calendar reserved for becoming better acquainted with ourselves, others, and God;

it is a time for . . . shared intimacies between Creator and creature. Our souls are replenished, quieted, nurtured, caressed. Rest without spiritual rest is incomplete."—Karen Burton Mains, from *Making Sunday Special*[13]

PART 2

Slow Down, Girl!

Chapter 8

FIVE DAYS AWAY

The Life-Review Retreat

When you picked up this book, the concept of taking any time away might have seemed like a stretch, and now you see I am inviting you to take five days away. I can hear your "slow down, girl!" And that's exactly what I'm saying to you: *Slow down, girl!*

Hopefully by now you've tried implementing shorter retreats and the Sabbath, and you found that God really showed up and used that time. Don't you wish you had more time away than just a couple days?

Girlfriend, let me tell you about the five-day "Life-Review" retreat. I know—the thought of that much time blew me away too when the idea first came to me. I can tell you, though, that it will take you to a whole new level with Jesus. And don't worry, I'll walk you through it.

In this next section, you'll read about my experience with five days away, what I did, how I used the time, and what I discovered. And I'll bring you along with me so you can see how it's done.

Five days away provides the opportunity to go deep with Jesus as you take a long look back at where your life's journey has taken you, where you are now, and where God might be leading you in the future. You might want to use the occasion of a life transition or a milestone birthday to consider this endeavor. A lot can happen in five days.

Since we aren't physically together, I can't pour you a cup of tea. But I have one, and I invite you to get one too, and settle in. Because I have a story to tell you.

The Backstory

My story isn't one of those headliners about some crisis that led to my long retreat. Rather, it was triggered by my waking up one day and realizing I was sixty years old. (Even as I write that, I'm thinking, "Who am I talking about? I can't be in my sixties already!")

Now, I hope to live to one hundred as long as I stay in relatively good shape; still, I recognized I was no longer in the middle of my life but closer to the end than the beginning. My grandchildren had started arriving, and I wanted to bequeath to them a solid package of wisdom and influence. I also wanted to see for myself the trajectory of God's work throughout my life, and reset for the next season. Alas, there were a few holes on my epic journey that I wanted to go back and fill in. Another overnight retreat was just not going to be enough.

As a self-appointed family historian, my life is well documented in journals and photos, but it felt more like a bag full of quilt pieces than an actual quilt. (I don't quilt, but you get the idea.) My longing to lay out all the pieces and discern the pattern and course of my life from beginning to end was emerging, but meanwhile the daily to-dos dominated my schedule.

The Invitation

In January 2011, I began to get the nudge: *It is time to go away.*

For a girl who dislikes being the slightest bit chilly, I wondered if I might just be dreaming during this cold Chicago winter. I was enticed, but with too many things to do and little energy to do them, I disregarded the whispers.

A week or so later, I woke up humming "Come Fly with Me." I had definitely not been listening to any crooners so I paid attention. *Might God be inviting me to come and spend time away with him? Is it finally the time to get away? If so, what was this notion of flying?*

Since my first "Getaway with God" personal retreat in 1977, I had returned more than fifty times for an afternoon, a day, or an overnight alone with God in a variety of settings, all no more than an hour from my home. This time, though, I got the distinct feeling that if I said yes to the nudge, I'd be going farther away than a retreat had ever taken me. I hoped I was right.

I love the ocean—not just in an "Oh, it is so pretty" kind of way, but with an intensity that started when I was four years old and walked for the first time in the waves on the Florida coast during a family vacation. The smell, the sight, the salty taste, the sound of the pounding waves, the feel of the wet sand on my toes captivated me and drew me back again and again from my Illinois home. By the end of February, the idea of a personal retreat at the ocean danced in my mind and began filling up pages in my journal. It was time to let my husband of thirty-eight years in on the plan.

I didn't give him much warning, just blurted it out: "Tom, I feel like God is asking me to come away for a personal retreat and to go to the ocean. I need to go before I turn sixty-one. I need to get away and see where I have been, where I am, and where I am going. I think I need at least four days. I have got to reset for the next season of my life. I am not at all done, but I'm not sure where I am going. It will take some time away to figure it out."

My husband listened quietly before responding. He is a marriage and family therapist, so he is a good listener. Finally he replied, "Why don't you just buy the tickets now?"

"What? You know that's not in the budget."

"Don't give up on this. Check the prices."

Stunned by his immediate endorsement, I jumped online. Not bad ticket prices, but they might as well have had extra zeroes as they still seemed out of reach.

Yet I couldn't get the retreat out of my mind. I needed to find a way. Believing that God provides the resources to follow his plans, I decided to ask him for three signs to convince me I was on the right track. I don't normally do this, but for this decision I needed extra confirmation.

The Confirmation

The very next day I met someone new at work who grew up in the exact area I planned to go. Sign number one—check!

That same night I experienced a vivid dream in which I purchased a needed item for my husband in the last seconds of a sale. The correlation to acting *now* for the retreat was clear. Sign number two.

On the lookout for the third sign, I sensed nothing that spoke to me throughout the whole next day. I'm embarrassed to say that I quickly went to *Have I missed it? Am I making all this up?*

God is so patient with me. In the evening my husband and I visited a residential center we were considering for my mother-in-law. In the midst of the tour, I had a strong urge to look out the window—just in time to see a large semi whiz by on the highway with one large word emblazoned on the side: YES.

I chuckled. Sign number three had just checked in. It was time to ask for the funds to go.

The Provision

Of course I believed God *could* provide for me. But *would* he? I bravely asked him to supply all the funds I needed for the plane tickets. Fares seem to shoot up without warning, and I wanted to be careful with his money. Within the next two days, from three different sources, some unexpected work for my self-employment business came to me, totaling the exact amount I needed. I quickly purchased the tickets. Now at least I was going somewhere.

All along I knew I wanted to stay at the lovely place on the Atlantic coast our family had previously visited a few times. Their website offered a free night with the purchase of three. Perfect. I just needed to pay for one night up front. Crazy as it seems, the next part of the funding showed up when my bank provided a generous bonus for opening a new account. I read over the fine print carefully, walked into the bank, and set it up. The bonus provided exactly the amount needed for one night and a discounted car rental for the whole trip.

In spite of all this provision, I still wondered how it would all come together. Oh me of little faith! Needing to cover two more nights, I continued to pray. The next time I visited the website, I noticed that the resort sponsored an essay contest to receive two nights free. I eagerly wrote a blurb about a fun memory of staying there. You guessed it—I was the winner.

In a very short time, God had provided my airfare, car, and accommodations without taking a cent from our family budget. My excitement built each day as my departure grew closer. Two days before I left, I received a gift of cash that covered the exact amount I had determined I needed for pocket money during my stay. Nothing had been overlooked in God's economy.

I knew now for sure that God had invited me, provided for me, and likely had a great plan awaiting me, although I wasn't sure what it entailed. My excitement about this retreat was off the charts. I had been away for weekend retreats before and once spent five days in Mexico speaking at a retreat there, but never had I taken five days alone with God. I couldn't wait to get to the beach, and I immediately started counting down the days till my departure. I also kept a running list of all the things I wanted to talk to God about while I was there—as if I would never have another chance to pray!

On Tuesday, May 10, 2011, I got up early to plant a few flowers left from Mother's Day. I set my away messages, added my last-minute toiletries and freshly laundered items. Then I climbed in the car and headed to O'Hare International Airport. The day had finally come.

Chapter 9

BEFORE YOU GO

Getting Ready to Get Away

I know you have probably taken a few trips before, but preparing for a long retreat has a few more components to it than just pulling out your suitcase.

Spiritual Preparation

Long before departure day, saturate your retreat with prayer. Consider modifying your regular prayer practices a week or two before you leave to focus on the upcoming retreat. Some concerns to cover are

- your health and your family's health;
- protection from accident or injury;
- a clear sense of day-to-day direction at the retreat;
- good sleep;
- no crises at home or work;
- a deepened sense of hearing from God; and
- anything else that is specific to your needs.

Enlist friends to pray for you for a week or so before you go and also for a few weeks after you return. My small group was glad to pray, but I wish I had asked them to start earlier as I hit a bump in the road before I left.

As with many spiritual attacks, I didn't see it coming. Eight days before my scheduled flight, I noticed I wasn't feeling well. I'm an "I'll be fine" kind of girl, so I kept on with the normal to-dos as long as possible. Then out of the blue—or out of the pit—a strange fever developed and hung on. No other symptoms showed up except fever-related ones such as lethargy. I couldn't stay awake.

I struggled to get work done, as I knew I would be taking a week off. But lacking energy, I wasn't very productive. Day after day the fever continued—for seven days.

I don't know what you think about the power of opposition to the things of God, but girlfriend, can you imagine how threatening five days with God is to the enemy of our souls? When this malady showed up in my body, I felt unprepared. I felt like an arsenal was unleashed to try to keep me home.

I wish I could sugarcoat this part of the story, but it may happen to you too. Maybe not a fever, but *something* will likely show up to deter you and cause you to second-guess the whole thing. Don't give in to fear.

The day before I left, the fever finally ceased. Due to my then-arthritic knee, I needed a cortisone shot in order to walk the beach, so I got that done. Then I pulled out my suitcase and started to pack. No other obstacles loomed. (By the way, I don't recommend waiting until the day before to pack. I was just too tired until then.)

Another part of spiritual preparation is to seek direction for specific Scriptures, themes, or even whole books of the Bible to focus on during your retreat. For a life-review retreat, you may discover that portions of the Bible that God has used in the past to speak into your life will come to the forefront again.

In addition, ask God to show you a loose or specific program for each day. For my retreat, I knew I was to spend a day on my past, another on the present, and a third on the future. I didn't receive anything more specific until I arrived, but those three agendas were enough for me to know I had a plan. I brought along a three-pack of white legal pads, one for each day. Legal pads help me organize my thoughts; you likely have your own preferences for tools.

Occasionally you may have no further direction than *go*, and the rest will become clear later. But while that might happen, assume that God will give you some guidance on how to use the longer time away before you leave. To that end, you might bring certain books or past journals along, but only if you feel led. Don't overpack.

For my five-day retreat, I was more impressed with what *not* to bring, such as a novel and magazines, so I wouldn't get distracted. I did bring two short books to aid in my retreat: a spiritual memoir and a health-related title.

I also brought an iPad to stay in touch with my family through email, but I knew my instruction was to check it once a day at 4:00 PM. How is that for clear guidance? That was the only time each day I ever used it. All my packing was intentional to keep me focused on the retreat; I wanted to avoid anything that might steal from this precious time.

One more thing: Spend time asking God specifically how to spend the first few hours. I would not have thought to go shopping on a retreat! (You'll read about that later.)

Preparation to Leave Home

While choosing your travel clothes is one part of getting ready to leave, there are other matters to consider as well. Not all of the following may apply to you, but take a look at these and see what else needs to go on your to-do list:

· Do you have any medical issues you need to be prepared for? Make sure you bring enough meds along, as well as any over-the-counter supplies you usually use. You may be able to stop and pick up something while away if necessary, but it's better not to be bothered.

· Do you have specific dietary needs to prepare for? How about preferences? I brought along favorite crackers, whole-wheat English muffins, and dark chocolate.

· Have you notified family, coworkers, neighbors, committee members, and any essential others that you will be away and unavailable?

· Will any bills come due for which you can set up payment before you leave?

· Do you have a journal with lots of blank pages?

· Do you need to rent a car? Book it ahead of time to get lower rates.

· Do you need to set away messages on your email accounts?

If you forgot something, don't let it bother you. One of the women who regularly goes on my small retreats actually enjoys forgetting something so she can have a little adventure to locate what she forgot.

what other women have to say

"Even though it's hard to get away from family and work, once you arrive at your retreat, you will be glad you are there."—Emery

Chapter 10

DAY ONE

"Now What?"

Did I tell you I'm a timid flyer? I usually choose an aisle seat so I don't have to keep being reminded I'm six miles up in the air. This time, though, I chose a window seat, as I didn't want to miss anything of the two-hour flight to South Carolina.

Upon arrival I picked up the car I had reserved. I tried to act cool, as though I did this all the time, but it was my first solo rental. I felt so grown up—until I got lost driving out of the airport.

The drive to my resort was beautiful, and I recognized many spots from previous visits. All was well until suddenly hail began to fall. Hail! I pretended to ignore it and walked into the lobby to check in. My balance owed for the four nights was $6.74 thanks to God's miraculous provision.

The hail continued as I pulled my bags into my room. Once I unpacked, I plopped on the bed to ponder the current events. I didn't think the hail was an attack, but I also knew it could turn into one if I fed the fears that were popping up. As I sat there, I began to thank God for every aspect of this trip—all the provision, the days ahead, the beauty of the landscape—and soon the hail stopped and the sun came out.

The ocean beckoned so I headed to the beach for a short stroll. The beauty was overpowering, and I continued my litany of thanks. Likely due to the storm, I was the only person at the shore, which added to the aura of the whole experience.

Before I left home, I had sensed God directing me to spend the first evening doing a few fun errands. Glad to oblige. I sensed his specific direction to go to my favorite women's retail store, Chico's, to buy a shirt to wear while I was there. I loved that idea but had no clue where to find a Chico's. But in obedience (a really *fun* obedience, I might add), I drove out of the resort. Right in front of me on the main road was a mall with, you guessed it, a Chico's store facing the highway.

I pulled in and right away saw what I was looking for. A long-sleeve, cotton, turquoise shirt that was perfect for a few days at the beach. I practically danced out of the store and headed to my next stop, a grocery store to stock up on provisions for my tiny kitchen. It felt as if I had a shopping buddy as I was directed to buy this, not that, to stay within my budget.

One last stop was to a casual but trendy restaurant to dine with Jesus before heading back to my room. I strongly sensed him sitting across the table and enjoying our date.

Errands done, it was time to go back and officially enter into my five-day retreat.

Now, I know you won't have the same plan at all, but let me share some principles I would encourage you to apply as you enter into your retreat.

Just as with a shorter retreat, take your time settling in, nose around, and orient yourself to your surroundings. Keep reminding yourself that you are *not* in a hurry.

I like to unpack my clothing into the closet and dresser to establish the feeling of staying awhile and make my clothes easily accessible. It is also fun to take time to arrange my books and such around the room to personalize it. Sometimes I bring a framed photo, candle, special cloth for the table, or whatever else I sense will help set the mood.

Once you feel ready to step into the retreat, create a ritual of it. You might have the whole day in front of you or it might be close to bedtime. Either way, officially open your retreat in a meaningful way.

Do you want to light a candle, sing a song, offer a prayer out loud? I like to pray the words Eli gave Samuel in 1 Samuel 3:9: "Speak, LORD, for your servant is listening." And then *listen*.

Isn't *being* so much harder than *doing* some days? Your retreat is a long stretch of *being* in the presence of God, with occasionally *doing* something as he directs.

Sample Schedule

I know you were probably hoping I would whip out a schedule again, so here you go. The following is a sample schedule for the first day of arrival, assuming you arrive late afternoon.

First Hour

Check in, slowly walk around the facility, unpack, and arrange your space.

Second Hour

Enter into your own "opening ceremony" with Jesus:

- Sing a worship song.
- Choose a psalm to read aloud. Some suggestions are Psalm 4, 16, 19, 25, 27, 29, 30, and 34. And that's just getting started.
- Pray aloud and commit every aspect of this time to the Lord. Include the weather, your health, your family at home, the work you left behind.

- Again speaking aloud, pour out your love and affection to Jesus, thanking him for bringing you to this point.
- Sing another worship song.
- Read a second psalm.
- Pray aloud all the desires of your heart for this retreat. Rambling is fine.
- Spend time listening for the still, small voice of the Holy Spirit.
- Write down what you hear.
- Finish with one more song and psalm.

Third Hour

Prepare for dinner. Consider changing your clothes to elevate your dining-with-Jesus mind-set. You might be in a public dining room, at a restaurant, or eating in your room. Be sure to say grace—and enjoy the food! Okay, this might not take a whole hour, so modify as needed.

Fourth Hour to the End of the Evening

Perhaps take another walk inside or outside, depending on the locale and weather. Is there a chapel where you can stop in? If you are at a monastery or convent, there will likely be evening prayers you can join in.

Spend time with a portion of Scripture. (See chapter 5, page 51, for ideas on where to jump in.) Picture the words being written just for *you* by substituting your name anywhere it says "you."

Did you bring an inspiring book along? Pull it out and read a chapter or two. If you are reading a devotional, such as *Jesus Calling* or *My Utmost for His Highest*, read or reread the section for today. These selections never fail to speak to me.

If you brought light bedtime reading or needlework, finish off the evening in that fashion. Avoid the TV and Internet, as they will quickly pull you out of your retreat zone. If something really news-worthy happens, don't worry; you will find out.

If you have a hard time falling asleep in a new place, just focus on resting, and whatever pops into your mind, turn it into a prayer. You might also add prayer for all the individuals you encountered today. You don't need to know their names in order to bless them; God knows who they are. Everyone played their part in getting you to the end of this day.

Tomorrow will be a full one, so ask God to prepare you during your sleep and direct your dreams.

what other women have to say

"Allowing God to nourish your soul benefits not only you but your family members and friends because it makes you a more God-centered woman. Jesus longs to spend time with you and bless you if you make the time and allow him to."—Janice

Chapter 11

Day Two

Looking Back

When it was time to plan my retreat week, I wanted to include May 11, as I always celebrate this date in some way as one of my "anniversaries of the heart." You have such anniversaries too, although you may not have defined them like that. Some of these dates were scheduled events; others started out as ordinary days, and then something magical emerged. I celebrate a few of these anniversaries each year and am always on the lookout for more. Because really, who doesn't like a celebration?

May 11 is the date when I received my first Communion at age seven. I remember so many details of that long-ago Sunday and treasure it as one of the best days of my childhood. So I always celebrate it. Never quite like this, though.

That day in South Carolina began just like at home, with tea and meeting with God for prayer and journaling time. But that is where the similarities to my home in the Chicago suburbs ended. Instead of my living room chair, I enjoyed sitting on my cute little balcony for my morning ritual and gazing at palm trees instead of elms.

The only direction I had about the rest of the day was a sense that it was about the past. Kind of a broad starting point, don't you think? I assumed God would reveal the details as the day went on. I was right.

After breakfast, I planned to rent a beach chair as I had done at this resort before, but when I called to ask the price, I was informed they weren't renting chairs yet. Problem. I contemplated jumping in the car to go buy a chair but felt God clearly leading me just to walk down to the beach, where he would provide a chair.

How will this work out? I wondered.

When I arrived at the beach, it was mostly deserted and quiet. There were, however, two attractive wooden beach chairs and an umbrella all set up on the sand. As I approached I noticed a reserved sign looped over one of the chairs. I walked around them a few times wondering who they were reserved for, as hardly anyone was around.

After a while, I began to wonder if they were reserved for me, just as I had felt God tell me. Gingerly I sat down, ready to jump up at any moment when the real owner came, but no one ever did. I finally settled in, feeling that I was in one chair while Jesus rested in the other.

The first thing out of my lumpy bag was one of the legal pads. Its blank, white pages stared at me, waiting for me to fill them. I confidently wrote "Past" on the first page and then sat back and waited.

Spiritual History: Early God Memories

At first I leaned back in my chair and let myself be lulled by the waves. Slowly I was drawn back to my early relationship with Jesus, starting with my first memories. Actually, I started with recalling my mother's stories of hearing me talk to Jesus from my bed. I guess he and I really were reviewing my whole life. I began to write all I remembered about my earliest awareness of him, my first prayers, my special religious medals and prayer books, smells and bells of certain worship services, Lenten observances, and stories about saints. I was surprised how fast it all came.

Do you remember the first time you felt a powerful response to God? I was fifteen and at a showing of the movie *The Greatest Story Ever Told*. As part of our religious education, my whole sophomore class attended.

I clearly recall sobbing at the end of the film, having finally understood that Christ died for my sins. Not such a cool move for an adolescent girl. Everyone else was ready to leave, and I was still frozen in my seat. The only response that made sense to me was to become a nun, so I was ready to sign up. Fortunately, someone along the way showed me that I had other options.

My spiritual timeline continued through high school and then seemed to shut down during the early college years. Like all of us, I needed to make my own choices about Jesus and not just be carried by my parents' dictates. At age twenty, after several years of wandering in my own wilderness, I made a decision to follow Jesus forever, and I have not swayed since.

As my writing slowed and I glanced back over the pages I had filled with memories, I realized how good it was to look at the history and see the continuity of God's role in my life.

For You . . .

You too have stories like mine, but of course the details will be different. Open your first notebook and begin your own journey of looking back. Take your time with this exercise and return to it when another memory pops up.

- What do you remember about your early relationship with the Lord?
- Were there particular places where you felt God's presence strongly?
- Did you have objects that helped you connect with him? Rituals in church or your home?

· Do you remember the first time you really responded to him? He does.

Spiritual Calling: Vocation

Finished with the history section, I took a walk on the beach and then came back to look at God's call on my life over the past sixty years. A big chunk of time, right?

Do you have any early memories of God getting your attention? I was about eight or nine and walking through my parents' bedroom in our home in Quincy, Illinois, when I became aware of God speaking to me. There was no audible voice, but it was a clear message all the same about my being an "influencer." I knew he was talking about using me to impact women and that it would involve speaking and writing.

Years later, during a group prayer time, an older woman that I highly respected had a similar message for me: "I think you will be an influencer."

Have you ever experienced something similar? A time when someone saw some strength or skill in you and spoke into your life? It gave a boost to what God had already revealed to you. Or perhaps it was the first time he brought it to your attention.

Another time, at a women's conference, I asked God to show me where I fit in the church. Immediately, as if I were watching a film, I saw myself perched on a branch of a large oak tree (pretty unlike me, as I don't like heights). In the scene, I was throwing down acorns to those who gathered on the margin of the tree but did not want to come closer. This defines much of my role in God's kingdom: connecting with those who are attracted to faith but not ready to commit.

Having these memories written down, all laid out together, was powerful.

For You . . .

God calls all of us to his service. No one is exempt. It is not his plan to keep you in the dark about how he would like to use you.

Even if you have lost sight of that direction years ago, it is still there. Sit quietly and get in touch with what you sense God is calling you to.

- Over the course of your life, what have been your favorite opportunities to serve?
- What area of service to God brings you the most joy or fills you with great energy?
- What are you doing that seems to have the most impact for others?
- If you could head up a service committee of your choosing, what would it target?

Write down what comes to mind. Of course, God is once again more focused on who we are becoming rather than on what we are doing, but he does have a perfect fit for us in his work on earth.

Spiritual Milestones: The Highlight Reel

"Where have we been together?" was the next question that rolled around in my head. Rewinding the video of my life to identify highlights of my relationship with God, I saw many.

My first memory of God's showing up in my life occurred when I was about five or six, when I found a near-dead baby bird. I brought the tiny creature home and put it in a shoe box to take care of it. In spite of my good nursing skills, the bird soon died. No one in my family seemed interested in its demise, so I planned a simple funeral which only I attended.

I buried the bird in my neighbor's yard for privacy from my parents and fashioned a small cross from a couple of twigs. The next day, when I went to pay my respects, on the grave was a shiny half dollar. I knew right away that God had given it to me to thank me for taking care of the bird.

You might have a story like that too.

The next episode I clearly remembered was when I was twenty

years old and spiritually searching. That would describe many of us at some point. Between my sophomore and junior years of college, without consulting my parents, I enrolled at Denver University to take a few courses and get away to the mountains. My mother was troubled by this decision and yet agreed to pray for discernment. Finally, she felt she needed to say yes to my going. This was unusual for her, since she was more of a naysayer.

My apartment was next to a chapel on campus called Evans Chapel. Later I found out it was named after John Evans, founder of Evanston, the town I now live in. I would visit the chapel in the evenings and, if it was empty, would literally lie down in the aisle and cry out to God to reveal himself to me ("if you are there," I always added).

One night after I exited the chapel, a young man approached me and handed me a leaflet called *The Permanent Revolution* about the transformation of the heart. I started to explain how the church had disappointed me, political demonstrations and protests had disappointed me, and I wasn't interested.

The guy (I never even caught his name) challenged me about differentiating between a relationship with God and a religion. As he continued to speak, his words began to make sense. I remembered my relationship with God from my youth and longed for that kind of intimacy again. I date my decision to follow Jesus to my encounter that evening, although it was slow to evolve over the summer. On the wall of my office there now hangs a photo of the chapel.

God broke through into my life many other times to reveal himself. I wrote about each encounter as I remembered it. Many of those incidents were amazing, such as the time I ran out of gas on a busy highway and a man with a full gas can "just happened" to show up. Others were more ordinary, such as a lost item turning up after prayer. But they all clearly showed the hand of God.

I recalled the day I met my husband. The first time I spoke to a group of women. Dreams I'd had for other people which brought them messages of hope. Like Mary in Luke 1:49, I could say that God had "done great things for me." I had a long list! As I sat on the beach that second day of my retreat, I felt full of his love and presence in my life.

For You . . .

Take time to review your spiritual milestones. As with Mary, God has done great things for you.

- Can you start a list of those great things? Go back as far as you can. Include something from this week.
- When you get stuck, ask God to show you what you forgot.

Disappointments

After spending time with my milestones of faith—those places of safety and strength—God told me it was time to look at my disappointments. I was not looking forward to it. The list came fast: the girls in grade school who excluded me, the first time I got my heart broken, my frequent feelings of being a misfit in high school, regular messages of inferiority—all came flooding back.

Disappointments from my mom and my dad and the too-soon death of my beloved grandmother pierced my heart. Work failures, deals that didn't come through, hoped-for financial success that seemed to elude me—all made the list along with deaths, friends' divorces, and missed opportunities. There were choices my children made or did not make, the loss of my last baby early in the pregnancy, friends who seemed to fail me, unfinished projects, and the many times when I myself had disappointed others. This was a difficult segment to complete.

Strolling there along the ocean shore, I held each memory for a moment to let myself feel its sting, then released it to the Father's waiting hands. It was my only way to clear my soul so I could move past the hurt. Each time an ocean wave rolled in and then receded, it seemed to take a disappointment with it. When I could remember no more, I felt cleansed and healed. Even at this writing, several years later, the freedom remains.

For You ...

Release your disappointments. Everyone experiences disappointments; God wants us to surrender them to his loving care so they don't hold us back. Invite him into a review of your life's disappointments. Let him lead the way through your memories.

- Do you sense any theme to your disappointments?
- Which disappointments felt out of your control?
- How about the ones you had a hand in?
- Do you need to forgive anyone, including yourself?

As each letdown runs through your mind, actually open your hand to release it. Trust me, you will feel so much better after handing it over. You don't need to be held back any longer.

Stuck Places

After reviewing my disappointments, I had hoped to move on to something more enjoyable. But God indicated it was time to review my stuck points: those times when I got scared and didn't want to move forward, or when he said *right* and I chose left, or when he said *stop* and I went on and ended up lost in a dark corner, not sure how to proceed.

I knew right where to start: third grade with Sister Marcella. I was bright and precocious and had something to say about everything. One day Sister Marcella asked another question I already knew the answer to. I wiggled in my seat and waved my hand furiously. But my teacher, ignoring my intense effort to get noticed, kept looking around the room to see who else could answer. I heard the other third graders mumble, "Oh, *her* again."

I was crushed and bewildered. Why were they saying those things? They might as well have said, "Shut up and sit down"—and that is exactly what I did for the next forty years. I have no memory of ever raising my hand again in class, all the way through college. I might have been called on, but I didn't want to risk being murmured about. A definite stuck point.

It wasn't hard to recall more. My fear of doing something wrong started early with an incident in my neighborhood that had unintended consequences. I have held back many times from moving forward in case I was wrong. You too?

Fear—not just of being talked about or of being wrong, but many other types of fear as well—kept me stuck. Fear of conflict or of intruding with my opinions into someone else's life kept me feeling safe but stuck. Shame about things I'd done or hadn't done made me sure I was disqualified from the really good stuff God had to offer. It was easy to see how often I, like the man in the parable who hid his talent (see Matt. 25:14–30), was afraid and wanted to play it safe.

I grieved there on the beach to think of how much more I could have done for God or been a conduit of his love, and of his gifts for others, if only I hadn't locked myself up. As each incident popped up where I had chosen to stay stuck, I once again repented and released it, clearing the way for what God wanted to do next.

For You . . .

Review your stuck points. While disappointments usually come to us at the hands of others, stuck points are often a result of our own choices. Ask God where you are stuck. He will show you. Addressing stuck points is like removing barriers from a road so you can continue at top speed into the life God has for you.

· Where in your life have you chosen not to move on? To turn back? To ignore God's leading?
· How have fear and shame influenced your choices?

Successes

It was time to take another walk on the beach. I was delighted to see that the chairs were still there. And having worked through my disappointments and stuck places, I was happy that we could now look at my successes—the points along the way when I said, "Yes, use me. I will go."

Donna, a single mom, and her daughters were the first ones to come to mind. I don't remember how we met as they lived in a different part of town. I spent time with them when I was a teenager, bringing them food or cash or just hanging out with them. Donna called me her best friend. I wish I had saved the letters she sent me while I was in college.

Loretta was the girl in school whom no one wanted to play with or even talk to. Remember cooties? Everyone thought she had them except me. I invited her to my birthday party one year. It was likely the first one she had ever been invited to. I was thrilled when she came to the door. The only problem was that she was a week too early! My mom and I both urged her to come back the following week on the real party day, but she did not. I don't know whatever happened to Loretta, but God does, and he assured me he saw my role in her life.

Have you ever heard of candy stripers? They were teenage volunteers at local hospitals who wore striped pinafores (really). I was a candy striper back in the day, which might have something to do with my current role as a hospital chaplain.

On the beach God showed me a particular patient with whom I had spent time and brought joy into her loneliness. An unhappy postmistress in a little town in Massachusetts was also a beneficiary of my kindness when I was eighteen. Many more stories came flooding in. It was fun to remember these incidents and to feel God's pleasure for being there in people's lives and serving them.

There at the beach, I stepped into a life review that included many people who have been a part of my journey, from one-time encounters to family members and close friends. I saw how my role in their lives made a difference. Sort of an *It's a Wonderful Life* moment without Bedford Falls. It was humbling and deeply satisfying.

For You...

Review your successes. This is the fun part. Imagine you are called onstage to celebrate your life. Everyone you have ever influenced in a positive way is stepping up to thank you. No room for disclaimers here; you deserve all the honor you are receiving. Enjoy this moment and write it all down.

- Whom do you see celebrating you?
- What are they saying?

Wrapping Up

It had been a long, productive second day of my retreat. I had faced and released my past pain and rejoiced in my lifetime successes. At the end of my time at the beach that day, I was able to summarize:

- I have seen God's hand at work in quiet and powerful ways throughout all my sixty years.
- He has a call on my life to serve him which has been confirmed at various points.
- I have acknowledged and let go of my disappointments.
- At many times I have shut down or turned away due to fear, shame, or feelings of inadequacy. I repented for all the times I could remember.
- I have imprinted on and influenced a lifetime of people.

God led me to Joel 2:19–29, which refers to a restoration of "the years the locusts have eaten" (v. 25) as well as a promise of "the autumn rains because he is faithful" (v. 23). The passage goes on to say, "You will praise the name of the LORD your God, who has worked wonders for you; never again will my people be shamed" (v. 26). At the autumn of my life, those were very powerful words.

I was finished for the day. I took a photo of the chairs to remember God's provision and then walked away. When I was only about twenty feet away, I turned back to look one more time; a guy with a little cart had come by to take the chairs down. The photo hangs in my office as a daily reminder of that amazing day.

For You . . .

Wrap up. Write a summary in your notebook of what God has shown you today. Maybe a particular verse will come to mind to help you process what transpired. Sit with God for a while to thank him for the day.

Day two is finished. Does a walk after dinner sound nice? You might want to spend time in light activity like reading or working a crossword puzzle, but take care not to immerse yourself in anything that will draw you away from your focus for these days.

Tomorrow we will look at the here and now, the present.

what other women have to say

"There is nothing like setting aside time and space to go to God with your deepest questions and longings, and giving him an opportunity to renew and refresh your spirit."—Missy

Chapter 12

DAY THREE

Looking Around

By the third retreat day, I felt as if I were in another dimension of time. I woke up with sweet memories of my day in the chair on the beach and amazement at the freedom I felt. How could anything else in the rest of the retreat top this?

God probably giggles when he hears such a question. If you've hung around Jesus for a while, you know he specializes in *more*. So my curiosity was piqued about what was next.

Do you ever have a hard time staying in the present? I can so easily flit back and forth from the past to the future and forget that the only moment in which we can fully live is the one we are in right now. Why is that so hard to remember?

Eager as I was to move on—oops, there I went again, jumping forward!—I knew God wanted to spend time with me in the moment, *this* moment, and show me some insights. Not just insights from the past (where I have been) or for the future (where I am going), but a deeper look at where I am right now in *this* season of my life. The focus of day three was the present.

But first I went out to breakfast. That part of the plan I knew all along.

Somehow I knew, before the retreat started, that breakfast this third day would not be in my little studio unit but in the restaurant on the property. Following Jesus is so much fun! Before I left my room, I grabbed another clean legal pad but kept it in the bag. Staying in the moment meant focusing on the beautiful array of colorful food options and not working through breakfast. So often I mindlessly eat while doing something else. You too?

Since even the directions for where to sit were so clear on the previous day, I wanted to follow God's leading again. After breakfast, I walked to the area beside one of the swimming pools, took a seat at a small table, and waited. (Be sure to ask God where he wants to meet you for your conversations. He is so marvelous in how he orchestrates the tiniest details.)

Pulling out the second blank legal pad, I wrote "The Present" across the top and again asked Jesus what he wanted to talk about first. He was ready. *Your dreams* popped into my mind. I knew he meant my night dreams.

Now, girlfriend, I am not one of those "dreamer" types. You know, those people who always have vivid dreams with tons of meaning. Not me. I usually don't remember anything from the night except how many times I woke up. In this season of my life, it is rare for me to sleep all the way through uninterrupted.

Remarkably, though, my dreams of the last few months seemed full of detail. It was such a surprising phenomenon, and I had started writing the dreams down in my journal each morning after they occurred so I wouldn't forget the details. Fortunately, I had the journal with me.

Following the theme from the day before of writing everything down, I listed all the dreams from my journal on my new legal pad, even if they didn't make any sense to me. Looking at them all together instead of one at a time, I could see what seemed to be a common thread running through them.

Besides recording my dreams, for some time now I had also been listening to God each day during my prayer time and, using my colored pens, writing down whatever I heard. Often a Scripture passage or clear word of encouragement for me to hold on to would come to mind.

So as I reviewed the dreams I had recorded in my journal in recent months, I also revisited the times when I thought God was speaking to me. With everything God said written in a different color, it was easy to thumb through the pages and look for the purple ink. Once again, I jotted down the highlights on my legal pad but didn't try to figure them out.

I wondered where this was going. Then Luke 6:38, a verse I had read that morning before breakfast, popped into my mind: "Give, and it will be given to you. A good measure, pressed down, shaken together and running over, will be poured into your lap. For with the measure you use, it will be measured to you."

What does that mean, God? Like viewing a partially finished jigsaw puzzle, I saw color groupings and border pieces, but the picture was far from complete.

I checked the time. I had someplace to go, so I wrapped up my pondering and set it aside for the moment. As with the leading to spend the first night shopping, I had sensed before I left for the retreat that I was to spend part of day three at a public garden about forty minutes from my hotel.

It was another pleasurable directive. The lovely drive inspired me— new scenery always does. Once I arrived at my destination, I grabbed my legal pad, planning to pick up where I had left off. But about ten steps from the car, I realized I had made an assumption and quickly checked in with God. Nope, this was a time to enjoy the beauty of the garden. So the legal pad got tossed into the back seat.

As I began my leisurely stroll, I felt like Eve in the first garden. The flowers and foliage were just coming into the fullness of spring. A sculpture of a young woman with flowing hair reminded me of myself at a younger age—and I felt much younger that day. I wandered around for a couple of hours, marveling at the Spanish moss, and snapped a few photos.

Why don't you take a little tour? I heard in a still, small voice. So I got in line with the couples, family groups, and clusters of friends for a pontoon boat tour of the garden's swamp areas. It might have seemed strange to the others that I was alone, but I wasn't alone at all.

After about three hours, a slow walk took me back to the entrance, and I whispered prayers of thanksgiving for the lovely respite. The time had come to return to the resort, and along the way I picked up a light lunch. Work was waiting ahead, but my refreshment tank was full from having spent time in nature.

I grabbed my legal pad and headed back to the beach in the late afternoon sunlight. I didn't expect to see the chairs again, but some nearby steps leading down to the ocean seemed fine for a workstation.

Back to my exploration of the present. My list of things to reflect on came quickly. Eleven areas called for a prayerful look at how I was doing right now. There was no science to how I determined each one; I just wrote them down as I thought of them. For each area I developed a few probing questions. Then I wrote down my answers, and I listened to God for how he wanted me to deal with each category. Was there an action he wanted me to take? Did he have anything else to say about a particular area? (Of course he did!)

If you're following the structure of my retreat for your own time away, take time now to create your "Present" list, and ask God for the main takeaways, the summary statements. No need to rush; see what emerges as you prayerfully wait. Here is my list for you to refer to. After each area I've provided the same questions for you to use that I asked myself.

Area #1: Health

This item wouldn't have made the top of my list a few decades ago, but in this season of my life, it gets top billing. My work as a hospital chaplain reminds me to take nothing for granted except grace.

For You . . .

- How would you rate your overall health?
- What steps are you currently taking to improve your health?
- How are you addressing any health concerns you might have?
- Are you satisfied with your food plan?
- What areas need attention in your health?
- What else does God want to say to you about your health?

Area #2: Family

Every one of us is related to someone. You may be a wife, mom, grandmother, mother-in-law, sister, sister-in-law, daughter, daughter-in-law, aunt, niece, cousin. How are you doing in your roles? Mine seem to be evolving. Adult children bring transitions, and the grand-children keep coming at regular intervals.

For You . . .

- What do you most enjoy about your family times together?
- Which of your family roles are most satisfying?
- What does your family need from you right now?
- What is the imprint you will leave behind for future generations?
- How do you think God views your family?
- Which areas need some attention in your family?
- What else does God want to say about your family relationships?

Area #3: Friendships

At this point in my life, I am rich in friends and enjoy a deep closeness with a handful of other women. This hasn't always been the case; isolation and loneliness sometimes seemed the norm. I thought it was another "just me" experience until I began to speak on the topic of friendship to women's groups and listen to some of the stories shared with me.

For You ...
- What do you like about your friendships?
- Are you satisfied with the quality of the friendships you have?
- In what ways could you be a better friend?
- Do you prefer a few close friends or a large community of friends?
- Is there anyone you would like to add to your circle of friends?
- What needs attention in your friendships?
- What else does God want to say about your friendships?

Area #4: Appearance

This might seem vain, but we care how we appear to the world, and as women of faith we are also representing God as we are out and about. Reminding myself again of Queen Esther's twelve months of beauty treatments, I freely wrote in this category, knowing it mattered to God too.

For You ...
- What do you like about your appearance? (Since we usually start with the stuff we *don't* like, I knew God was in this question.)
- What is your ideal style of clothing? (Interesting question, don't you think?) Does your actual clothing fit your ideal style? Why or why not?
- How do you feel about your hair?
- When was the most recent time your appearance best represented your authentic self? What were you wearing?
- What needs attention in your appearance?
- What else does God want to say to you about your appearance?

Area #5: Church Involvement

If you are reading this book you likely have had some relationship to a church. Are you currently part of a church? If not, would you like to be? While I have been part of the same church for more than forty years, I need to keep re-choosing it at life intervals. I change, the church changes, and we keep needing each other. There's no perfect church, only a perfect God who helps us work out the kinks.

For You . . .

· What is your connection to your church like at this point?
· How do you think others at your church see you?
· Do you need to get more invested? In what areas?
· Do your gifts fit your roles at church?
· What needs attention in your church involvement?
· What else does God want to say about your relationship to your church?

Area #6: Home

Each of us lives somewhere. We are responsible for our home care even if we have help with the chores, be it paid or unpaid. How is the atmosphere in your home? Does it create an environment for individuals to thrive? If you have children, what do you think they will remember about their home when they're grown?

Acts 17:26 reminds us that God knows where we live: "From one man he made all the nations, that they should inhabit the whole earth; and he marked out their appointed times in history and the boundaries of their lands." So he cares too about the space around us. Did you ever think about the fact that most of our God encounters occur at home?

For You . . .

· What do you like about your home?
· Do you have a favorite room?

· Do you feel you manage your home well?
· How do you do with order?
· How do you think others feel when they are in your home?
· In what ways do you use your home for Jesus?
· What needs attention at home?
· What else does God want to say about your relationship to your home?

Area #7: Ministry

We all have a ministry, the place where our calling meets the world's need. Frederick Buechner defines ministry this way in his book *Wishful Thinking*: "The place God calls you to is the place where your deep gladness and the world's deep hunger meet."[14] Call it as you see it; don't make it too complicated. You might not know all the specifics, but you know you are an encourager, or a helper, or an organizer. Trust God to continue to use you along those lines, and wait for more opportunities.*

For You . . .

· In what ways does God primarily use you to benefit and serve others?
· We are all called to be salt and light and the fragrance of Christ. We are to shine like stars of the universe. How's that going for you in your circles?
· Where do you feel nudges these days to do something?
· Has your ministry changed through your different life seasons?

---

*God has given each believer spiritual gifts that can help and bless the body of Christ. If you haven't done so already, you might take an inventory to see how God has specifically gifted you. Your church may have a test that is available to you. If not, a good online resource is the Team Ministry Spiritual Gifts Inventory, https://gifts.churchgrowth.org/cgi-cg/gifts.cgi?intro=1.

- What needs attention in your ministry?
- What else does God want to say about your ministry?

Area #8: Work

"Whatever you do, work at it with all your heart, as working for the Lord" (Col. 3:23). This applies if our work is caring for our children or running a corporation. Many of us change our jobs throughout the course of our work lives. Take a look at your circumstances right now.

For You . . .

- What do you like about your work?
- How is God using you there?
- How do you think others see you at work?
- What keeps you from working "with all your heart"?
- What needs attention at work?
- What else does God want to say about your relationship to your work?

Area #9: Community/Neighbors

Jesus said the second greatest commandment is to "love your neighbor as yourself." I'm sure he meant our neighbor next door as well as the wider call to love anyone you happen to meet along your journey.

For You . . .

- How many neighbors on your block have you had a conversation with?
- How many have you served in some way?
- How do you think your neighbors view you?
- What kind of impact would you like to have in your community?
- Are you praying for your community leaders?

- What else does God want to say about your relationship to your neighbors and community?

Area #10: Finances

Everyone has finances to deal with one way or another. Like the stock market, you may have experienced a lot of ups and downs over the years. Use this opportunity to look at where you are financially, not to try to actually solve any issues. After the retreat, you can find many financial books and helps if you need them. Looking for something specific? Check out Dave Ramsey's many resources.[15]

For You . . .

- What is working well in managing your finances?
- If you have debt, do you have a plan to get out? How long will it take you?
- Do you have a plan for savings? Is it adequate for your goals?
- What is your plan for giving?
- What is the next step you would like to take in your finances?
- What needs attention in your finances?
- What else does God want to say in relation to finances?

Area #11: Projects

This might seem a funny category, but I have a number of big projects going—from putting my photos into albums, to organizing family memorabilia, to finding ancestors online. I love doing these projects but keep putting them off, or I make a good start but then don't get back to it for months. I want to honor God with my time and my projects.

For You . . .

- What are the household or fun projects you keep putting off?
- Are the projects on your list things you really need or want to

get to, or can you let them go? Why are they important or not important?

· What would it take for you to finish one of your projects?
· What needs attention with your projects? What small things could you do in the next few months that will help you complete a project?
· What else does God want to say about your special projects?

Wrapping Up

As I sat on those wooden steps by the beach, I looked over my sheets of paper again and wondered how they all fit together: the dreams, the direction, the lists of present reflections. Like one of those hidden-picture puzzles my grandchildren love, what God wanted to show me became clear as I simply looked at the present season in my life.

Have you ever been to a wedding where there was a "charge" given to the bride and groom? The purpose of these words to the couple was to remind them of their duties and responsibilities in love toward each other.

My friend, God has a charge for you and me, and he is eager to give it to us. Usually that happens during our life transitions. At this point in my retreat, I began to feel the stirrings of a charge from God to me for my next season. Two points became clear: (1) I was to give myself away to others with abandon, and (2) I was to tell my story.

Not quite like the Ten Commandments written on stone. But I knew now that I would leave the retreat with a clearly defined life list which would shape my remaining years. But I'm getting ahead of myself.

I went back to my room for the rest of the evening and a light dinner. I got to bed early, as I hoped to make it down to the beach the next morning for the sunrise.

Tomorrow would be back to the future—the place I thought was my starting point.

what other women have to say

"You don't know what a gift you are missing until you experience a personal retreat."—Sally

....

Chapter 13

DAY FOUR

Looking Ahead

Watching the sun rise over the ocean is one of my favorite things to do. Words cannot describe the splendor of the minute-by-minute change of hues on the horizon as the sun crawls out from the night sky. I have witnessed a few sunrises over the years, and I couldn't wait to see this one down on "my" beach.

I had only one problem: I detest alarm clocks. Yeah, I know, we all do, but I decided years ago to train myself to get up without one and only employ it on days when I have to catch an early plane or train. Even on this precious fourth morning, as much as I wanted to see the sunrise, I didn't want to wake up to a shrill alarm. So I asked God to wake me so I wouldn't miss the morning's glory. And of course he did. It was so dark that I needed to use the flashlight on my phone to find my way down to the beach.

The preview of coming attractions was just beginning to roll across the sky as I arrived. A vivid panorama of purple, red, then fuchsia, followed by orange lit up the sky. I started snapping photos but then decided I would rather just view the sunrise than

....

record it. So I tucked the phone in my pocket and let myself be mesmerized.

After about an hour of the spectacle of light, the beachcombers began to head down, so I meandered back to my room to reset for the day. My last full retreat day at the ocean lay before me, and I felt like I had so much more I wanted to do. Where to start?

I knew this day was finally all about the future, the agenda I started with on the first day until God revealed his other intentions. I loved what transpired all the other days and realized how foundational it was for this day. Still, I was glad to finally get to look ahead. What was next? I sure hoped I would have a plan by tomorrow.

After a lovely time on the lanai with Jesus to start my morning in the usual way, I was ready to hit the beach again with enough snacks to qualify for lunch. Based on the previous two days, I wasn't sure what the seating situation would be once I got down there, but sure enough, the chairs were now all set out to be rented. I lined myself up for one and plopped down, just as I had planned on the first day.

What Do You Want?

I pulled out my last new legal pad and wrote, "The Future" like I was starting a science fiction novel. So many juicy possibilities for what might fill these pages.

"Okay, Lord, what's the plan?" I asked.

His response was not what I expected: *What would you like the future to look like?*

"*Me?* What do *I* want?" Believe me, that was not a hard question. Like many of us, I had sort of a "permanent" prayer list that I prayed day after day, year after year, decade after decade. I knew the future I wanted.

But if he wanted to hear all those things again I would oblige. I quickly listed the desires of my heart for my family, my work, my ministry goals, getting out of debt, maintaining good health, and living to be one hundred (in great shape!) alongside my husband. Then I threw in a few trips I would like to take. Why not? He asked me what I *wanted.*

For You . . .

You too have a future that only God can see, and he invites you to have a hand in shaping it. How would you answer the question "What do you want?" He is asking you too. Take some time with this. It is a fun exercise.

· What are your heart desires for your family's future?
· What would your ideal ministry look like?
· What could life look like on the other side of debt?
· What kind of ideal lifestyle do you see for your next stage in life? And the one after that, all the way to your eighties and beyond?
· Any trips or adventures you're hoping for?
· What if nothing held you back from this day forward?

What Does God Want?

Do you really believe this can happen?

That was God's next question for me. I sensed I needed to answer it before anything else could transpire. (Have you ever noticed how, in the Gospels, Jesus sometimes asked people, "What do you want me to do for you?" before he healed them? This felt similar.)

"Yes!" I practically shouted. Faith is a strong gift for me, and anyway, doesn't God say, "I am the LORD, the God of all mankind. Is anything too hard for me?" (Jer. 32:27)?

After I showed him the list, so to speak, I sensed that he too thought it was a good list. How I sensed this isn't something I can adequately describe, but I felt not just God's approval but also his satisfaction. He seemed to say it was "very consistent" with his calling. Good to know, right?

So I decided to ask him a question, not just to be polite but because I really wanted to know. "What do *you* want, God?" I was kind of afraid of what he would say.

Crazy as it is, a lot of us, in the back of our minds, expect God to answer that question with the one thing we ourselves for sure *don't* want. I think you know what I'm talking about: *Don't make me go to* (fill in the country). *Please, don't ask me to be a* (whatever it is you dread). Stuff like that. You can probably relate. Where does that come from?

So after I blurted my question, I held my breath and waited . . . but only for a second. He had a list for me too, and it wasn't what I expected. I reminded myself he was the one who said that if a child asks his father for bread, the father is not going to give him a stone (see Matt. 7:9). Indeed, no stone was offered, nor was it a to-do list. It was a to-be list.

For You . . .

- What do you think God wants for you going forward?
- Is there a consistency between what you want and what you sense God wants for you?
- Is there an area he has been nudging you about?
- How can you cooperate with God for the future he has planned for you?
- Do you hear him saying anything else? None of this is supposed to be a big secret.

Becoming a Woman God Can Fully Use

After I asked God my "What do you want?" question, the first item I sensed was: *I want you to take the rest of your ten talents out of the bag and start investing them now.*

Whoa. I had read that parable of the talents many times. In Matthew 25:14–30, Jesus told the story of three people who received money, or talents. One Bible translation calls them "bags of gold."

One guy received ten, one got five, and the last received one talent. The first two invested their talents, while the last guy decided to play it safe and bury his. I already visited this story in chapter 11 when referring to "stuck points." The one who buried his gift displeased his master. The implication is, we are to fully use whatever God has given us. I was beginning to feel convicted.

I first encountered this parable when I was a child, and I must admit, it always bothered me how hard Jesus was on the one guy who buried his talent. He was trying to be careful, right? Didn't want to do anything foolish. I can relate.

Well, I was glad to hear I had a full supply of talents to begin with. But I wasn't aware that some of them were still rattling around in the bag. Of course I was curious to know which ones I wasn't using. Or maybe I knew.

Invest them. Hmm. Where? How?

The future is a lot about fully using all God has given us.

Before I could fully process this, God had something else to say: *I want you to assume you are one-hundred-percent available to me all the time until I call you home. I want you to glorify my name in your kitchen, your yard, your bedroom, your car, your desk, your podium, your pager, and your phone.* That about covers it all, doesn't it? My home, my family times, my connection with neighbors, anywhere I go; when I am writing, speaking, at the hospital as a chaplain, and on the phone with my coaching clients.

Of course I thought I was already pretty good at some of that. He wouldn't have brought it up if I was so stellar, though. What would it look like if I took it up a notch or ten? If every time I left home, I intended to glorify Jesus wherever I went? If that's what was on my mind whenever I stepped into my yard? If *all* of my interactions started with him? How would that shape the future? Looking at it from his perspective, I saw a lot of holes I wanted to fill going forward.

For You . . .

- Are most of your "talents" showing up in your life, or are some still in the bag?
- Listen to see where he would like to use you to glorify his name. Any surprises?
- How are you doing with being "one-hundred-percent available"?

Your Role in Your Long-Term Future

The kicker came next: *Most of these things on your "this is what I want" list are the result of your choices and actions.* What? I thought everything either happened or didn't according to God's plan. Somehow I thought my role was rather passive. Praying, believing, and trying to show up in the right place at the right time. Is there more?

Suddenly, as if the proverbial lightbulb went on, I saw how my choices and actions helped shape the eventual outcome of just about everything I covered yesterday in my life review. We weren't looking at the present anymore but far ahead.

Take my health, for example. I had declared that I wanted to enjoy optimal health and live to be one hundred. Did I think that was going to happen just because I wanted it to, and meanwhile I could eat Cheetos and doughnuts and it would all work out? (I don't, by the way, but you get the idea.)

Yes, of course God has the ultimate last word. Acts 17:26 talks about how he knows the "appointed times" set for us. But our choices help determine the outcome. When I eat right and move often, I have a much better chance of fulfilling my desire to be in optimal health. Same goes for you.

Another area: What kind of financial future was I looking for? I had told God I wanted to be debt free, have some savings tucked away, and regularly give to my local church and other causes I support. I'm sure that's what he wants for me too. But will that all just happen? Am I free to spend as I please because God's got it covered?

My choices determine part of the outcome here too. I have learned the hard way (more than once) that in the realm of money, hoping it will all work out isn't the savviest plan.

How about with my family? What kind of future do I see for them, and how can I shape it while still deferring to God's plans? The way I talk to my family, prioritize time with them, and bless them overall has a huge effect, not only on them but also on future generations. God is really big on setting things up for people not yet born.

Same with my work. I show up at the computer and do my work whether I feel inspired or not, and many days it is more "not." What happens after that is up to God, but I must make the choice to take my place at the desk and write, edit, submit, resubmit, research, and do all the work involved in putting words in print. His plan, my choices.

God showed me that even with all his amazing provisions for my retreat, the funds came in because I took action steps. I still had to write the essay for the resort in order to win the prize, walk into the bank and sign up for my two hundred dollars, and do the work so my writing would be available for purchase.

You see, girlfriend, the future isn't just ten years down the road; it starts in the next minute and plays out the rest of our lives. God is ready to reshape our future—a future that only he can see—but he needs our cooperation.

My morning with God, focusing on my future, went on to other specific areas, personal areas just for me, during the afternoon. But it's time to turn to you.

For You . . .

- Spend some time now with Jesus and give him every aspect of your future. Only he knows if you have a day or ten thousand days ahead of you, but he wants you to serve and glorify him in every one of them.

· Are you excited about your future? Does it look any different from a few days ago? How so?
· Finish up this reflection by thanking God for the day and seeing if there are any more insights he wants to give you. Don't rush.

Wrapping Up

As I sat in my chair on the beach, the family next to me pulled out a kite. Now, you don't know this, but the symbol of a kite has had deep significance for me since my children were teenagers. I laughed at God's humor of revealing to me that he was with me in that moment, securing a future for me that was as unique and meaningful to me as the kite.

For You . . .

How would you like to end this day of focusing on your future? Maybe take a walk. Enjoy a nice dinner. And in any case, celebrate what God has done during these days.

Tomorrow the retreat ends, but there are still a few things you need to wrap up.

---

what other women have to say

"You are the only person who can create the space you need to nourish yourself with a retreat. You never know what God will do once you step into a space where it is quiet enough for you to hear him."—Julie

---

DAY FIVE

Reentering the "Real" World

Day five, the last day of my five-day immersion, arrived right on schedule. Though I knew I was faithful to follow the plan God had shown me for the previous days, I was in no hurry to leave.

No sunrise today, but the beach beckoned early, so once again I grabbed my camera and headed down for a last, long walk along the shore. With sadness, I recognized that it would be awhile, perhaps a long while, before I would be back on an ocean beach, so I tried to "seal in" the sound of the waves, the scent of the salt, the sight of the whitecaps breaking on the sand. I know you can find music with such sounds, but it isn't the same. My camera kept clicking till I put it away so I could really focus on what was right in front of me.

As I slowly walked back up to my room, I prayed about how to use these last hours. I intentionally had booked a later flight so I could finish the retreat unhurriedly rather than rushing off. The five days had gone by in a flash, yet it seemed like ages since I was home. What kind of "closing ceremonies" could I create to wrap up this life-changing time?

Do you like symbols and ceremonies? You might not be wired that way, but I am a rituals kind of girl, and I knew some symbolism would be meaningful for me. But what? As I waited for direction, it began to come. I decided to review each day by rereading my notes, starting with "The Past." Once again I gave thanks to God for releasing me from my past disappointments and stuck places.

I knew there were some points of the past I never wanted to revisit again. (Do you have those too? Of course you do.) How could I signify that I had left those memories in the past once and for all? This might sound crazy, but I grabbed a roll of toilet paper and wrote some "lowlights" of my life, one per sheet, and then ceremoniously flushed the sheets away with a triumphant note. Done!

After that little ceremony, I returned to the notes. I paged through it as I would a scrapbook, celebrating once again the highlights and successes of the past and laughing with delight at some of the amazing people and events I have experienced over the years. Reframing the past through God's eyes was powerful.

Next up: "The Present" review. I absorbed my observations and the renewed decisions I had made for my current season of life. How could I hold on to them in a tangible way?

A large apple I had been waiting to eat suddenly looked inviting. I interrupted my reading to cut into it and noticed the unusually large seeds.

The seeds!

I counted them. There were enough for each area of my life I had reviewed during my "present" day. Coincidence? I don't think so. I gave each seed a name, such as "friendships," gathered them up, and went outside on a short walk. Like Johnny Appleseed, I cast each one onto the ground as a reminder that I wanted to plant what God showed me that day. I don't expect apple trees to start showing up on the property, but if you see one in about ten years you'll know how it got started.

One area remained: "The Future." How could I signify it?

The whole time I had been at the ocean, I had not gone fully into the water but only waded along the shore. On this last day, I wanted to feel the water on my face, a baptism of sorts into the new life I wanted to grow into for the rest of my days.

I hustled down to the water again and walked toward the waves instead of alongside them. As the salt water splashed on my face, I asked God to renew me for the future that only he knows. I asked for wisdom and self-control for the choices ahead to bring my cooperation to what he wanted for me in the days to come. I came out of the water feeling transformed.

One hour to go before driving back to the airport. I knew I had enough time but felt like every minute counted. Each day at the beach resulted in some tangible wrap-up points that I had written out at the end of the day. One more time I opened all three legal pads and pulled out the action steps from each section. These were specific instructions God had given me to follow from now through the rest of my life. Twenty-one steps total.

I'm sure you would like to hear some of them, right? Some steps were between God and me, but here are some samples I can share with you. They might even become yours.

1. *Deliver what you promise.* I am great at promising but have not always followed through with excellence.
2. *Take a window seat.* That one came from the first day on my flight down, when God reminded me that the best seat might not always feel like the safest or most convenient.
3. *Tell your story.* Girlfriend, you're reading it.
4. *Take the rest of your talents out of the bag and use them all.* Easier some days than others. It usually requires keeping both hands in use; sometimes I feel as though I have one tied behind my back, and I slow down too much.

5. *Give and it will be given to you.* I often ask God to remind me of this when I feel "giving fatigue"—and it's rarely about money.
6. *Eat fewer carbs.* This might be a Tish-only one, but probably not.
7. *Maintain order at home.* Some days I'm still working on achieving order in the first place, never mind maintaining it, but I'm making progress.
8. *Linger.* Sometimes—okay, often—I am in too much of a hurry in a conversation. Jesus didn't seem to have that problem, so I hope he can help me with it.

You get the idea. I wrote down my action steps in the order they showed up in my notes, knowing I would return to the list often.

Done. At last I felt I was finished. My experience at the ocean had been a truly mountaintop one. Now nothing was left to do except pack up, check out, return the car, and get on the plane.

The flight was quick. My husband swooped me up, and we went directly to a birthday party for a young friend. Life was back on. Was I ready?

Returning Home

You may not have a birthday party to go to on the way home from your retreat, but once your bags are packed, your thoughts will turn to what awaits you.

- What did I miss on the home front?
- Are there any crises brewing that no one told me about?
- What came in the mail?
- How many phone calls will I have to return?
- What happened to the projects at work?
- Is there a mess waiting in the kitchen?
- I hope nothing big happened.

Here are a few tips on how to return to your daily routine while preserving the spirit of the retreat.

Thank Those Who Stepped In for You

Most likely, your family, your coworkers, maybe even your neighbors all played a supporting role while you were gone. Someone picked up your slack, covered for you, and did more than their share so you could be away. Be sure to thank them sincerely. Sometimes all you need to say is, "I so appreciate your helping out while I was gone," without going into a lot of detail.

Keep It Light

If possible, don't schedule much for the day you get home. I read once that you need a day to recover for each day you were gone. That may not be possible, but you get the idea. It is easier to slip back in after a day or two away, but try to keep your schedule light.

If you are taking a two-day retreat, can you be gone Friday and Saturday instead of Saturday and Sunday so you have a day before going back to work? If you are the primary grocery shopper and meal planner in your household, can someone else pick up a few things so you don't have to dash right to the store?

Preserve the Quiet

You probably did minimal talking while you were gone, and sometimes the rush of noise can be overwhelming. Instead of slipping back into listening to music in the car, ballgames on the radio, and the blaring TV in the family room, see how long you can go without turning anything on.

Can the phone calls wait for a little while? Of course, you will need and want to talk to your family and close friends, and if you have kids at home, you will likely do a lot of talking. But see if you can start small when reengaging with media and everyone around you.

All will be waiting in a few hours or a few days. Everything might sound louder at first.

Follow Through Immediately

Often on a retreat God will speak to you about a specific action or response to take when you return. One of my action steps from my five-day retreat was to eat fewer carbs. There wasn't a particular diet I felt led to follow, but I got the idea. It seemed important for me to adjust my food intake right away, so I started with my next meal.

On my recent twenty-four-hour retreat this spring, God spoke to me about getting up at 6:00 AM five days a week in order to write (as I am doing at this moment). I returned home on a Thursday night, and the next morning I was at my desk by 6:00 AM. I followed that pattern for several months without ever setting an alarm. Had I decided to wait until the following week to begin, I think you wouldn't be reading this book.

Of course, God might have given you specific instructions for something that would occur in the future instead of right away. Stay on the lookout for those events or circumstances to show up.

Did God ask you about a relationship? Did he direct you to set an appointment or have a conversation with someone? Make a note to put it in motion in a few days, once you are resettled.

Tell the Story

No doubt many in your circle will be fascinated by the idea of taking yourself away for a multiday retreat. You will likely get deluged by questions: "How was it?" "What happened?" Some people will just be curious. Others will really want to know, as they are part of your life's journey and your prayer team. Perhaps some are considering taking a retreat themselves and want to hear your story to help shape their own decision.

It's okay to feel some hesitancy about sharing. You might feel your story is sacred, and you don't want to reveal the details to just anyone. Don't expect everyone to "get it" even after you share a few specifics. When in doubt, ask Jesus what to share and whom to share it with for their benefit.

Of course, if you're married, telling your husband about your encounter with God is something you will want to do, and he will want to hear the details. My husband and I had talked briefly every day while I was gone, so he was up to date on the layout of each day. When I got home, I gave Tom a brief summary on the way to the birthday party. And we set aside a block of uninterrupted time for me to open my notes and tell him the story of what God had done. My closest friends and my women's group also got a full report.

And now, years later, I've shared it with you.

Follow Your Action Steps

The twenty-one short action steps God gave me during my time away were specific instructions for when I returned home. All were one-liners that popped up at different times in various settings. For instance, as I got out of my car after visiting the public garden, I sensed, *Don't be afraid of what you see or hear.* I was uncertain what that meant for me then. But many times since, I have repeated those words to myself as I see or hear things that can stir up fear.

The day after I got back, I reviewed the list again and reorganized it in a way I could more easily remember. Then I began committing it to memory. I keep a copy in my prayer journal and another in my wallet. When I wake up in the middle of the night, sometimes I will pray down the list until I fall back asleep.

Of course, this is no substitute for reading God's Word. However, my list offers words of life to me; each entry pushes me toward the fullness of life God has planned for me. I still pray over the items every day.

Jesus knew that revising my list was a perfect follow-up for a list maker like me. But it might not happen the same way for you. Trust his leading.

Deuteronomy and Joshua include references to the Israelites gathering "stones of remembrance" to remind the people of what God did in their midst. My list of action steps as well as the visible lineup of seashells in my office are part of my stones of remembrance. I also assembled a photo book that I keep in sight in my office. And remember my story of the two beach chairs? I have enlarged my photo of those chairs, and it now hangs on my wall as a constant reminder of Jesus's desire to spend time with me.

Plan Your Next Retreat

Creating a rhythm of retreats in your annual calendar can go a long way to preserving the intimacy with Jesus you'll discover once you've taken your own first getaway. You may be in a season where an annual retreat of even just one day feels like a stretch, or you may be able to pull away more often. You will know. Mark your calendar with something vague like "next spring" if setting a definite date seems too elusive right now.

For several years following my long retreat, I took a twenty-four hour-retreat in May. Later I invited a few other women to come along on short retreats several other times each year to introduce them to the experience (see appendix D for more details). In 2016, it was the five-year mark of my long retreat, and I went back to Myrtle Beach for another five days.

These suggestions are just some of the ways I and others make the transition back from the retreat to the normal day-to-day routine. One thing to keep in mind: The enemy of our souls will try to rob you of your joy and steal the truth of what God said and did during your time away. Keep vigilant in your prayers and watch out for the attack. And "don't doubt in the darkness what you've seen in the light," as the saying goes. This is especially true after a retreat.

After a time away of any length, I can feel my intimacy with Jesus lingering in my daily interactions. A new level of focus, clear-headedness, and confidence replaces my anxious thoughts. You will likely have a similar response, with your own flavor to it. I'm sure my family notices too (with gratitude) that my reserves for the normal frustrations of life last longer after I have been away with God.

The retreat is a starting point for what comes next, not an end in itself.

A Few Final Thoughts

Throughout our long conversation, I've offered a buffet of ideas on how to get away with God. We've looked at short-term retreats as well as longer, more intensive times away. We also explored the Sabbath, which gives us a retreat every single week without our ever having to leave home.

You may already be dashing off an email to make a reservation for your own retreat. Or maybe you are still uncertain about the whole thing. Either way, you're thinking about it, right? That has been my intention all along.

Here's one more thing to consider. It comes directly from Scripture and shows what a retreat *can* feel like.

How priceless is your unfailing love, O God!
    People take refuge in the shadow of your wings.
They feast on the abundance of your house;
    you give them drink from your river of delights.
For with you is the fountain of life;
    in your light we see light.

(Ps. 36:7–9)

I love the language of that psalm. Refuge. Feasting. A deep drink from the "river of delights." Sounds wonderful, doesn't it?

Jesus is inviting you, as he did his disciples, to "come with me by yourselves to a quiet place and get some rest" (Mark 6:31).

He will meet you there and show you what's waiting.

RSVP yes!

A final PS: I would love to hear from you about your retreat experience after reading this book. You can email me at Letitia.Suk@gmail.com. Thank you!

what other women have to say

"We often separate body and spirit during the day, and personal retreats are wonderful, necessary ways to unite those two again so we can live as whole, connected people."—Cheryl Lynn

APPENDIX A

Optional Retreat Exercises for Any Length of Retreat

I have attempted to give you a lot of detail on the how-tos of structuring your retreat. But if you are a very concrete girl like me, you always want a little more.

Here are the retreat exercises I provide for the women who come on guided personal retreats with me. Feel free to adapt them for your own use, and fit them in at any point of your retreat.

1. **On My Mind:** Brainstorm the things you need to take care of sometime. Don't worry about categorizing, just list whatever pops up. I do it on paper, but any format is fine. Here's how it works:

   A. Gather supplies. I love to use a fresh white legal pad, and I bring a new one to each retreat. The only other requirement is a blank calendar, which you can draw or easily make on your computer. I found a monthly planner at the dollar store and bought three at that price.

   B. Get comfortable and settle in with a cup of something and some nice music.

   C. Start emptying your mind onto the paper. Pay no attention to the order—that comes later. My own list might include these items:

   · Find a missing sweater.

   · Buy a new shower curtain.

   · Order a baby gift.

   · Make a blog schedule.

- Get photos printed.
- Update Goodreads.
- Come up with a new plan for housework.
- Think about a summer trip.

D. Take a break. Walk around, fill your cup, and then come back to the list.

E. By each item write D (do), B (buy), or P (plan). Later you could break those down more if you like, such as *Call, Order, Make.*

F. Pull out the blank calendar and start meshing your brainstorm list with the calendar for a rough draft. Later you can transfer the plan to your real calendar. Not everything must be done this week or this month. For example, I need to buy train tickets this month, but planning a summer trip can wait until March. I'm going to Target this weekend, so I will get the shower curtain. Sundays would be a good time to update Goodreads. Sometime in April I will get back to a creative project.

G. Keep the list handy to update. Cross off tasks as you complete them.

H. Repeat in a few months or whenever you feel the need. Usually by then the list is somewhat crossed off and ready for a redo.

2. **Look Back:** Think back over the last few months or further. What were the dominant themes? What showed up that surprised you? Was God speaking to you about something in particular? If you keep a journal, that would be a helpful tool for this exercise. Flipping back through your calendar can work too. Stay with this for a while and see if you detect any patterns.

3. **Add/Let Go:** What do you feel God asking you to *add* to your life right now? It might be a spiritual discipline, a course of study,

food choices, a relationship, exercise, more sleep and rest, or some life-giving pursuit. In order to make room for whatever it may be, what do you need to *let go of*? The snooze button? Mindlessly surfing the web? TV? Your comfort zone? A volunteer activity you're no longer called to? Don't rush through this exercise.

4. **Personal Inventory:** This exercise is a mini version of the guided contemplation of your present as detailed in chapter 12. Take a close look at each of these areas, and ask God how he sees them and whether he has any action steps for you. Before you begin, give thanks for each area.
   A. Health
   B. Family
   C. Friendships
   D. Appearance
   E. Church involvement
   F. Home
   G. Ministry
   H. Work
   I. Community/neighbors
   J. Finances
   K. Projects

5. **Look Forward:** What do you feel called to in the next few months? How do you think your life will look different by the end of the year? In five years? What part of this is your responsibility? What part is God's?

6. **Ten Goals in Ninety Days:** Ninety days is a good amount of time to invest in changing your life. It is a short-term commitment, yet long enough to make a difference. To do this exercise, think over different areas of your life and pinpoint what actions

over the course of the next ninety days would bring satisfying and realistic results. Many life coaches use a variation of this exercise; here is mine:

A. Make a rough draft of all the goals that might work for this exercise, and pick the ten that seem the most doable and rewarding. Choose your start and end dates.

B. Ideally, choose a mix of goals that can be accomplished in a short time and others that will take steady attention. For example, clearing out a closet might take all of one day, but it can be completed in that time. Conversely, completing a chapter or two of a book you've dreamed of writing will probably take the full ninety days.

C. Make sure your goals are measurable. For example, "Eat healthier" is not measurable, but "Eat fish twice a week" is. Similarly, "Read the Bible more" is vague, but "Read one proverb every day" is specific.

D. Decide which form of accountability will be most effective for you. Consider posting your goals in a prominent place, and review them with prayer each day. Enlist a close friend or relative to check in on your progress. And keep a special notebook for your goals so you can detail the results. For example, if you decide to take a walk every day for the next ninety days, make a chart listing each day and log where you walked and for how long. Hiring a life coach to work alongside of you during this process can not only hold you accountable but also help you break through any barriers that come up.

E. Enjoy the process, and get ready to change your life!

APPENDIX B

How I Changed My Picture of Prayer

In chapter 5 I suggested creating a photo prayer journal. I wrote this article, "How I Changed My Picture of Prayer," which was published in *Today's Christian Woman* magazine (September 2008). I include it here in its entirety.

For years, my prayers were scattered. I'd start with the crisis of the day, then mentally spin off to groceries I needed or calls I had to make. Then I'd nod off for a short nap, and wake with the resolution to "pray harder" next time.

That all changed the day I leafed through a stack of family photographs and found myself praying for each person pictured. As I looked at my children's smiling, hope-filled faces, asking God to bless and protect them felt effortless. I prayed he'd put their dreams within reach, strengthen their relationships to him, and keep their hearts and actions pure.

This time I couldn't *stop* praying.

The next day I grabbed the photos and designed a system to motivate me in prayer.

I bought a small scrapbook and pasted a photo of a specific person on each left-hand page. On the corresponding right-hand page, I wrote broad prayer request categories of how I wanted to pray for that person.

I designated the first spread for me. So next to my smiling portrait, I listed all the ways I want God to work in and through me—to help me obey his nudges, be the best wife possible, maintain healthy relationships with my children, and spread Jesus's love. Then I listed themes: health issues, church involvement, work goals, financial integrity, and other big-ticket items.

I placed my husband's photo on the next spread. As I looked at him, I was easily able to focus and pray down my list: for his passion for God, for his mentoring of our children, for his wisdom and discernment at work, for his continued spiritual growth.

Next came my children. I created a different prayer list based on each child's unique personality. But I gave them all common themes: a strong relationship to God, wisdom for life choices, purity with the opposite sex, preparation for marriage and work, and involvement in Christian community.

After the family pages, I designated spreads for our extended family, my church small group, and a few close friends. The last section was for current prayer requests: the couple who were getting married, the guy from church who was fighting brain cancer, a friend's daughter who was struggling with her faith. And often when people would ask me to pray for them, I'd say yes and ask for a photo. There in the back section, that photo would remind me to actually keep my promise.

The photo prayer journal has helped me focus on asking God to do bigger work in each individual's life, not just help on a math test or heal a cold. I keep the lists short—limited to what seems important for the particular season.

This prayer method is great because I can use it while I'm spending time with God in the morning or while I'm standing in line at the grocery store. Waiting for an appointment or even sitting at a long stoplight is enough time to cover a page or two. Whether it's a quick run through the list or a longer, more focused prayer session, I connect with God for my family in whatever time I have available.

I've used this journal for more than a decade now. Each fall, I rewrite the lists and update the photos. And every day, I still get excited to open this book and start praying.

Appendix C

Additional Prayer Models

ACTS Prayer Model

- *Adoration.* Praise and worship God, read psalms to him, and speak words of love.
- *Confession.* Admit what you have done or not done that separates you from God.
- *Thanksgiving.* Thank God for everything and anything that comes to mind.
- *Supplication.* Ask God for what is on your "need" list today.

"Be Still, and Know That I Am God"

Take time to focus on each word.

- "Be still, and know that I am God" (Ps. 46:10)
- Be still and know that I am.
- Be still and know.
- Be still.
- Be.

The Jesus Prayer

This prayer is from the sixth century: "Lord Jesus Christ, Son of the living God, have mercy on me, a sinner."

- Try inhaling as you pray, "Lord Jesus Christ, Son of the living God."
- Exhale on "Have mercy on me, a sinner." Stay relaxed and breathe slowly.
- Repeat.

Breath Prayers

Similar to the Jesus Prayer, any couplet prayer or Scripture can be adapted to the inhale/exhale format:

- "Speak, LORD, / for your servant is listening" (1 Sam. 3:9).
- Lord Jesus / I trust you.
- You are / in control.
- Give me your peace. / Take my fear.

Palms Down/Palms Up

Sit quietly with your palms resting on your thighs. It is impossible to hold anything on the tops of our hands. Release in prayer anything that is troubling you. Take as much time as you need. When you are ready, turn your palms up, indicating you are ready to receive God's peace, blessing, and grace. If you find your cares returning, repeat the exercise anytime.

Prayer Walk

Once you are comfortable in your surroundings, choose an area of prayer for a segment of your walk—say a city block. Then switch to a new topic for the next block. I used to pray for each of my children block by block.

Written Prayers

Writing prayers down helps you to focus and also to look back on the results. I have been writing prayers for years and listening for any response God might have for me. A friend suggested using different colored inks for my prayers and God's responses so I can more easily locate the conversations later in my journal.

Proverb of the Day

There are thirty-one chapters in the book of Proverbs, and thirty-one days in many months. Pray through the chapter in Proverbs that corresponds with the date.

APPENDIX D

Designing a Group Personal Retreat

Even though I strongly encourage women to go off on their own retreats, I have found that introducing them to the concept of a personal retreat in a small group setting has been very successful. Small groups provide a community setting to personally experience the presence of God. Although most of the time the women are on their own, the group gatherings as well as the mealtimes provide a place for processing and conversation. A group retreat can be a great first step for someone who is interested in a personal retreat but likely won't try it on her own. After an initial group retreat, many women feel confident to take the next one alone.

My foray into small group retreats began when I sent email invitations to eight women to join me at a local retreat center to spend twenty-two hours together for a retreat I called "Slow Dance with Jesus." The invitation read like this:

I am planning to host a guided personal retreat for six to eight women on [date] and thought you might be interested. I have taken more than fifty personal retreats and find them very transforming. I want to invite other women into this life-giving experience.

I am planning on starting Friday night at 7:00 PM in a local retreat center and ending around 5:00 PM on Saturday. You will mostly be on your own, with three to four short group times. Cost is $[amount] and includes your room and two meals.

This retreat has no specific agenda, only you spending extended time with Jesus to pray, plan, nap, look at the upcoming season, or take walks. For those of you who sign up, I will offer some possible themes for you to follow.

I have attached handouts on some different themes to consider as well as logistics on what to bring and how to structure your time.

The RSVPs began to come in. The testimonials in the previous chapters are from these women, reflecting on how powerful the retreat experience was for them.

If you would like to try this model, I've included the following steps to get you started.

1. Choose a small group to invite and set the date and times.
2. Reserve a local venue. Usually I do this at least three months ahead of time.
3. Create a registration form and ask for a deposit by a certain date. On the form, in addition to the women's names and contact info, ask if they have any food allergies so you can notify the venue. I also ask what is attracting each woman to the retreat. That gives me a sense of how to best guide the time.
4. Create handouts on retreat themes and send them to the registrants. Use the material in this book as well as a suggested list of items to pack.
5. Design a schedule for the time, including a few short group sessions and direction for personal time. See below for a sample schedule.
6. Engage the participants by sending a reminder and last-minute logistics such as parking info and directions to the location.

7. Prepare folders for each participant with the schedule, optional retreat exercises from appendix A, and a map of the facility if available.
8. Consider bringing along little gifts for the attendees' rooms. Recently I bought a single rose, battery votive candle, and dark chocolate to welcome each woman upon her arrival to her room. It was a hit.
9. Arrive at least an hour before the retreat begins to pray over the space.
10. Move through the retreat and plan to stay on schedule.
11. After it is over, ask for feedback for the next time.

Sample Schedule for "Slow Dance with Jesus" (Twenty-Two-Hour Retreat)

Friday

7:00 PM: Group gathering for welcome and intros, as not everyone knows each other. (Besides name and season of life, this can include prompts such as, "Tell us something you would like us to know about yourself" or "What are you hoping for during this time?")

7:45 PM: Bedtime. Time alone with optional exercises provided (see appendix A).

Saturday

7:45 AM: Optional morning group prayer in lounge

8:00–8:45 AM: Breakfast (silence optional)

8:45–9:15 AM: Group gathering for devotional reading, prayer for the day, explanation of exercises

9:15–9:45 AM: Optional "How to Create a Prayer Journal" workshop (see appendix B)

9:15 AM–12:30 PM: Time alone with optional exercises provided (see appendix A)

12:30–1:30 PM: Lunch (silence optional)

1:30–4:00 PM: Individual meetings with the retreat leader if desired (sign up on sheet in lounge)

1:30–4:15 PM: Time alone with optional exercises provided (walk, nap, or the list from appendix A)

4:15–5:00 PM: Group wrap-up (stories, prayer, wrap-up remarks)

5:00 PM: End of retreat

In participant folders, I provide the following information.

how should I use my time?

Friday Night

Spend some time just sitting with Jesus and enjoying small talk. Don't worry about telling your whole story. Just get acquainted or reacquainted. *Don't rush.*

The following activities may be useful:

❖ Write a prayer of dedication of the time to God. Ask the Holy Spirit to direct your thoughts and responses during the retreat.

❖ Try one of the prayer models (from appendix C).

❖ Spend time with a portion of Scripture that is life-giving to you. Just a few verses are fine. I like Ephesians 1, Psalm 18, Romans 12, or John 15. Just pick one to start with.

❖ Develop a practice of moving *slowly* throughout the time. Walk slowly, respond slowly, eat slowly. Settle into his pace for you to experience rest.

❖ Invite Jesus to sit in the chapel with you. See what comes up, but try not to force an agenda.

❖ When you get back to your room, get comfortable and ask him what is on his mind for the weekend.

❖ Imagine you are chatting with Jesus and getting a checkup. Let him know how your body is feeling, what's filling your mind, your concerns about the health of your family, and anything else that bubbles up.

❖ Write out your "On My Mind" (from appendix A).

❖ Consider the "Look Back" exercise (from appendix A).

❖ Sing a worship song or read aloud from Psalms, if you feel stuck.

❖ Get ready for bed slowly and start your rest, if you are feeling sleepy.

Saturday

8:45–9:15 AM: Group gathering

9:15–9:45 AM: Optional "How to Create a Prayer Journal" workshop, or time alone with the following optional exercises:

❖ Start by inviting God's presence with you and committing your time to the Lord for his purposes. Wait a few minutes before moving on to enjoy the quiet.

❖ Start with your usual morning spiritual practices, if you have not yet done those. Enjoy each segment without hurrying.

❖ Meditate next on a portion of Scripture. Sometimes I have picked that out ahead of time; other times I feel God leading me somewhere in the Word right then. I usually choose a different passage from my daily Bible reading plan just to mix it up. Plan to stay with this for at least twenty minutes.

❖ Try another one of the prayer models (from appendix C).

9:45 AM–12:15 PM: Now that you are settled and have dedicated your time to Jesus and spent some time in the Word, move into the theme of your retreat, or consider one of the following exercises:

❖ "On My Mind" if you haven't already done it, or else the "Personal Inventory" exercise.

❖ If you are on a restorative retreat, now might be time for a morning stroll to find some beauty in nature. See what signs of God you can find on your walk.

❖ If you came to listen to God through his Word, pull out your tools. Did you bring a Bible study along? Time to jump in. Did you plan to do an inductive Bible study? If you're studying a biblical character, did you choose someone well known or more obscure? Why do you think you were drawn to this person? How would you like to approach that study? List the person's attributes, and place yourself in the story. Reflect on what it would be like to be friends with this person.

❖ Are you taking a planning retreat? Use this morning time to lay out the pieces of your life and ask God how he would like to rearrange them. "Every morning I lay out the pieces of my life on your altar and watch for fire to descend" (Ps. 5:3 MSG).

❖ Are you prayerfully making new goals? Can you get a rough draft done before lunch? I like to start with all the possibilities and narrow them down to the ones God seems to be highlighting. Plan to refine them in the afternoon. See the "Ten Goals in Ninety Days" exercise (from appendix A).

If you have a little time before lunch, take a walk; otherwise, save that for the afternoon.

12:30–1:30 PM: Lunch. The lunch break can also include a walk around the facility.

Thirty-minute afternoon appointments can be made with the retreat leader.

1:30–2:30 PM:

❖ Ready to get back into your primary agenda? This might be a good time to take another portion of Scripture to study, or pick up where you left off in your biblical theme or character study.

❖ Goal setters, start getting specific using the SMART goal model: specific, measurable, attainable, realistic, time-bound.

❖ Looking to be refreshed? Is art on display at the center for you to view? Did you bring some beautiful music to enjoy? Maybe you brought a beautiful picture book to indulge in.

2:30–3:15 PM: This is a good time for an afternoon break. If you haven't taken a longer walk outdoors, do it now. Come back to a cup of tea from the snack area if possible. Resist the urge to check for emails or voice mails unless you are in the middle of an emergency.

3:15–4:00 PM: Begin to wrap up your day. Finish any Bible studies you may have started. Recopy your goals and pray over them. Take a look at the calendar you created and commit your time slots to God.

4:00–4:45 PM: Group gathering for stories, prayer, wrap-up.

APPENDIX E

How to Find a Retreat Center

M any venues work well for a personal retreat: a hotel, a bed-and-breakfast, a cabin in the woods, even your friend's home while she is away. Some women are successful at using their own quiet homes, but most of us would be too distracted.

Following are some Internet links for retreat centers. Many of the centers are Catholic, but people of all faiths are welcome. The list is not exhaustive; however, each site provides an array of locations nationally and even worldwide:

> http://www.retreatfinder.com (not all faith-based; use search field to find "Christian")
> http://www.findthedivine.com (click "retreat centers")
> http://www.catholicretreats.net (put "private" in the search field)
> http://jesuits.org/retreat-centers
> http://www.osb.org/retreats
> http://www.monasteries.net
> http://www.goodnightandgodbless.com (international)
> http://tatfoundation.org/retreat_centers2.htm (mostly small cabins or hermitages)
> http://runhardrestwell.com (individual and group retreats)

NOTES

1. Ben Campbell Johnson and Paul Lang, *Time Away: A Guide for Personal Retreat* (Nashville: Upper Room Books, 2010), 31.
2. "The Discipleship Journal Bible Reading Plan," The Navigators, 2005, https://www.navigators.org/www_navigators_org/media /navigators/tools/Resources/Discipleship-Journal-Bible-Read ing-Plan-9781617479083.pdf.
3. Anne Ortlund, *Disciplines of the Beautiful Woman* (Nashville: Word Books, 1984), 52.
4. Johnson and Lang, *Time Away*, 83.
5. Richard Foster, "What Is Spiritual Direction?" *Christianity Today*, February 4, 2009, http://www.christianitytoday.com/ct/2009 /january/27.30.html.
6. Selections from the Book of Common Prayer can be found online. One good website is The (Online) Book of Common Prayer, http://www.bcponline.org. The URL for the "Order for Compline" is http://www.bcponline.org/DailyOffice/compline.html.
7. See http://livingforwardbook.com/resources/.
8. Lynne M. Baab, *Sabbath Keeping: Finding Freedom in the Rhythms of Rest* (Downers Grove, IL: InterVarsity Press, 2005), 11.
9. Wayne Muller, *Sabbath: Finding Rest, Renewal, and Delight in Our Busy Lives* (New York: Bantam, 2000), back cover copy.
10. Karen Burton Mains, *Making Sunday Special* (Nashville: Word Books, 1987).
11. Keri Wyatt Kent, *Rest: Living in Sabbath Simplicity* (Grand Rapids: Zondervan, 2008), 108.
12. Marva J. Dawn, *Keeping the Sabbath Wholly: Ceasing, Resting, Embracing, Feasting* (Grand Rapids: Eerdmans, 1989), 183.
13. Mains, *Making Sunday Special*, 115.
14. Frederick Buechner, *Wishful Thinking: A Theological ABC* (San Francisco: HarperOne, 1993), 118–19.
15. See http://www.DaveRamsey.com.

ABOUT THE AUTHOR

Letitia (Tish) Suk invites women to create an intentional life centered in Jesus. She loves to speak and write to women of all ages about establishing life-giving spiritual practices and celebrating family life.

The author of *Rhythms of Renewal*, Tish blogs at http://hopeforthe best.org on chasing the intentional life. She also serves as a guide for personal retreats and is a certified life coach and an on-call hospital chaplain.

Tish encourages and inspires women to live the abundant life Jesus offers. Recognizing that there are different seasons of life, she offers practical tips for moving through each season with grace and laughter.

She and her husband, Tom, live in the Chicago suburbs and are parents of four grown children. Find out more at http://LetitiaSuk.com.